| Praise for *Unpack Your Impact* |

Unpack Your Impact delivers a profound and fresh perspective on cultural integration in social studies classrooms. It equips readers with meaningful and tangible methods to have honest discussions while exploring topics that have been desperately missing from traditional textbooks. Personally, my favorite aspect of the book is that LaNesha and Naomi present eye-opening ways to provide historical meaning across various subjects.

This work's appreciation of the importance of the "M" in STEM lessons (mathematics) was a unique addition that I personally connected with. Even though the focus was on elementary education, I found it to be inspirational at all levels. Also, as a new parent, I found that the themes presented opportunities for families to engage in this work. This book is a must-buy!

—Dr. Valerie Camille Jones, mathematics specialist
and Presidential Award winner

LaNesha and Naomi have done it again! As educators, they understand what steps are needed to help teachers rethink their practices. The duo continues to push educators to do better for ALL kids!

—Vera Ahiyya, educator and book curator

I've had the privilege of bearing witness to the phenomenal work of both Naomi and LaNesha and am beyond excited about this book! This is what I wish I had in my early years of teaching. It is practical, inspiring, relevant and needed! I encourage all educators to read this book and learn from two of the absolute best!

—Shaun Woodly, PhD, author, educator, speaker, and
founder of the movement Teach Hustle Inspire

Naomi and LaNesha completely transformed their classrooms into places full of culture and joy—and in this book, they teach you to do the same!

—Kyle Schwartz, educator and author of *I Wish My Teacher Knew*

This book is written for primary educators, but anyone in the educational field will benefit from reading it. *Unpack Your Impact* challenges educators to take a look at "what's always been done" and ask themselves: Who is this lesson serving? The lessons and conversations that these teachers share in the book will fascinate you.

—Nicole S. Turner, author of *Simply Instructional Coaching: Questions Asked and Answered from the Field*

For years, O'Brien and Tabb have been consistent with their message about creating a classroom that establishes self-efficacy for students from all backgrounds. After the unfortunate death of George Floyd, America was forced to look at institutions that have allowed racism to wreak havoc for centuries. Contrary to popular belief, the education system isn't immune to enforcing those toxic beliefs that are rooted in racism. In this amazing book, LaNesha and Naomi have carefully detailed how educators and families across the world can begin to broaden their impact by unpacking archaic methods that are no longer useful. I know you will enjoy it!

—Michael Bonner, educator and author of *Get Up or Give Up: How I Almost Gave Up on Teaching*

What an indescribable feeling it is to anticipate great learning from one you taught yourself. Usually the chip off the old block follows the path of the block. However, since I transitioned to teaching as a mid-life career move, I find myself learning from and following the lead established by my daughter LaNesha. Her partnership with Naomi has given me new insight, strategies, and methodologies. I am excited to share their stories and implement their ideas.

—C. Nickerson Bolden, author of *Indiana Avenue* and *Bridging the Gulf*

There are a few voices in my life that I highly regard. LaNesha Tabb and Naomi O'Brien are two of those voices. But what I wasn't expecting when I picked up *Unpack Your Impact* was how deeply it would move me. Not only will this book remind you of the importance and value of anti-racism teaching and social studies instruction, but it will have you reevaluating the way you think about all sorts of things. Buy a few copies because you'll immediately want to pass it along to others you know.

—Todd Nesloney, director of culture and strategic leadership, TEPSA, author

Unpack Your Impact is a groundbreaking look at the way social studies should be taught—authentic, culturally relevant, and anti-racist—in the elementary grades and beyond. With its mix of concrete ideas, anecdotes, and self-reflective questioning, this book is necessary for every elementary school teacher who has thought, "I don't have time to teach social studies" (which is just about all of us). LaNesha and Naomi prove that students are never too young to begin developing democratic ideals about community, citizenship, and equity. You are guaranteed to finish this book with newfound knowledge of not just teaching social studies but revolutionizing how social studies is taught.

—Adam Dovico, author

Unpack Your Impact

NAOMI O'BRIEN & LANESHA TABB

UNPACK YOUR IMPACT

How Two Primary Teachers Ditched
Problematic Lessons and Built a
Culture-Centered Curriculum

Unpack Your Impact: How Two Primary Teachers Ditched Problematic Lessons and Built a Culture-Centered Curriculum
© 2020 Naomi O'Brien and LaNesha Tabb

This book is available at special discounts when purchased in quantity for educational purposes or as premiums, promotions, or fundraisers. For inquiries and details, contact the publisher at books@daveburgessconsulting.com.

Published by Dave Burgess Consulting, Inc.
San Diego, CA
DaveBurgessConsulting.com

Library of Congress Control Number: 2020944278
Paperback ISBN: 978-1-951600-48-8
Ebook ISBN: 978-1-951600-49-5

Cover and interior design by Liz Schreiter
Editing and production by Reading List Editorial: readinglisteditorial.com

To my parents, C. Nickerson and Kimberly Bolden, thank you for the love, support, inspiration, and foundation upon which I stand.

—LaNesha Tabb

To my husband, sons, friends, and past students, thank you for the support, love, and inspiration.

—Naomi O'Brien

Contents

INTRODUCTION

As primary-classroom educators, we hold so much power. We lay a foundation for more than literacy and math skills. We help in preparing students for a lifetime of learning, curiosity, perspective, empathy, and respect—all of which depend on what we decide to teach our students. Every decision that we make as educators can shape how our students see the world and learn to interact with others. Yes, our students' parents and guardians bear a huge share of this responsibility, but there's no denying the significant role of educators in students' lives.

As we've reckoned with the huge extent of this power and responsibility, our mission has become to help other primary teachers unpack the impact we all have in our primary classrooms. The way that mission has evolved is the story we'd like to tell through this book. It's a story that begins with our own—LaNesha's and Naomi's—careers as teachers.

We want to explicitly state that as we discuss terms around culture, inclusion, diversity, and history in this book, we will inevitably get some things wrong. We might read this book one day in the future and cringe at a term or activity that we've shared. We are okay with that. We are on

a journey to be better each day as we learn more and more. We don't mind failing forward and admitting that we needed to evolve in our thinking. Even within the time frame of writing this book, we've had to go back constantly to tweak and reword things so that we expressed ourselves to the best of our ability. We know that we won't get it perfect, and we know that no one will ever be perfect in this kind of work. Even so, we hope you hear our hearts as we share our journey.

————

For years, many of us teachers were beaten over the head with data—data from standardized testing, data that told us that across the nation schools were failing at teaching math and reading. Then the new millennium brought a new acronym with plenty of buzz (because we educators love us a good acronym): STEM. It exploded. There were conferences, blog posts, YouTube videos, and more, all focused around this idea of inserting engineering principles into instruction. We were told that we had to get our students prepared for jobs that didn't even exist yet.

We saw teachers embrace STEM with a passion. In our own classrooms, we brought in buckets of trash and told kids to create robots from them; we launched objects across the room; we built structures strong enough to hold eggs, basketballs, and even students. We learned how to ask, imagine, plan, create, improve, and collaborate. And—honestly—it was fun. At the time, we needed some fun.

We felt a shift happening not only in our country, but our classrooms. The 2016 election season was an intense time to watch the news or scroll through social media. Every headline, article, and viral video in circulation seemed to have the same underlying goal: polarization. It was enough to watch this play out on social media and the news, but when this energy started to trickle down into the schools, we began to worry. We heard a news report about children leaving school because other students chanted political slogans regarding the "building of walls" at them as they walked to class. We remember when a news channel interviewed a local award-winning BIPOC (Black, Indigenous, and people of color) robotics team that had been verbally insulted and told to go back to where they "came from" after winning the grand prize at a middle school competition. We even overheard our own kindergarten students discussing some of the public figures and events that they had heard on television. "If you vote for such-and-such, that means you hate America," one child exclaimed. With every passing news cycle, we noticed that our elementary students were not only becoming aware of things happening in the political arena but were already being affected by them. We realized we were not prepared for the intensity of the conversations beginning in classrooms with students as young as five years old. That's when it hit us. We were missing social studies. Real social studies.

We love the explanation of the subject given by Margit E. McGuire in "What Happened to Social Studies?" that social studies is "more than reading for comprehension. It is learning powerful ideas that demonstrate how social systems work, in the past and in other places, whether next door or around the world. The teaching of social studies should be organized around powerful ideas, and these ideas must be revisited from multiple perspectives."[1]

Thinking back on our own educations, we couldn't recall learning social studies topics from multiple perspectives. There was typically one narrative, and our job was to learn it, memorize it, celebrate it, and be proud of it.

We can see the consequences of an education like this when we ask people what happened during a particular war or movement and they all say similar things. Here's an example: We follow lots of elementary school teachers on social media, teachers of all grades—kindergarten, first, second, third, fourth. One October, as we were scrolling through Instagram, we saw post after post after post about pumpkins from teachers across many grade levels. We were struck by a question—Do teachers ever stop to consider that kids could possibly engage in a small

---

1 Margit E. McGuire, "What Happened to Social Studies? The Disappearing Curriculum," *Phi Delta Kappan* 88, no. 8 (2007): 620-624.

variation of the same old pumpkin unit year after year? We shared these thoughts with a friend of ours, and she actually said, "You know, there have been times when I have cleaned out my second grader's backpack and my kindergartener's backpack and the schoolwork has been very similar." That gave us chills.

Year after year, students are getting the pumpkin unit, the apple unit (you're not going to teach first grade and not teach Johnny Appleseed), the turkey unit—and heaven help us if we don't teach our gingerbread unit! So many educators are teaching the same topics and themes year after year. (There is absolutely no judgment coming from us. You are reading a book written by two teachers who used to LOVE a good Johnny Appleseed unit.)

While those topics can be fun, we are missing out on so many other opportunities—and those are fun too! We want to be extremely clear: it's not that we are against pumpkins, apples, shamrocks, or any other thematic unit that makes elementary school fun. We are, however, against *only* teaching pumpkins, apples, and shamrocks. We want to encourage teachers to expose students to as many impactful, interesting, and beautiful ideas about the real world as we can. Why would we continue to teach the same old themes when there is a whole world of more ideas?

So, against the backdrop of one of the most intense political seasons we'd witnessed, we felt it was critical to not only start teaching social studies but to teach it like we had never seen it done before. We immediately began to brainstorm, and we decided to make a list of qualities that we would hope to find in the "perfect" social studies curriculum. Faster than we anticipated, ideas like the following were spilling out of our heads:

- Develop a structure to study *tons* of cultures, focusing on diversity.
- Expose students to history, sociology, economics, geography, and civics.
- Revisit well-known heroes and stories from history *and* discover the missing voices and narratives of lesser-known stories.
- Find a way for students to share and celebrate their own cultures.
- Represent inventors, scientists, mathematicians, etc., from different cultural backgrounds.
- Get students to practice civil discourse, focusing on perspective and empathy.
- Create global learners who would be exposed to real-world concepts.

And here's the thing: we wanted to do this kind of work in the primary grades. Because why not? We firmly believe that little kids can do big things—it's all about the delivery.

We began to build and teach lessons for our students in Denver (in Naomi's classroom) and Indianapolis (in LaNesha's), and we were amazed for a few reasons:

1. Social studies went from being nonexistent to quite literally our favorite part of the day. The conversations. The ideas. The questions. The globes. The ENGAGEMENT.
2. Students began to expect it. We heard this in small, quiet ways: "Mrs. Tabb, when are we gonna learn 'world stuff'"

again?" or "Which kinda people are we learning about next week?" In their six-year-old vernacular, our students were asking when we'd study geography and culture again, because—apparently—they hadn't had enough.

3. Parents and guardians were responding. We were getting emails and messages like, "I usually pick Morgan up before her brother, and she normally asks to play with my phone in the car. Today, we talked about the US government for the entire car ride. Wow."

After teaching this way for three years, here is what we can tell you: it was the most fun we'd had in a really long time. Teaching real topics is invigorating! We also revel in the idea of teaching students true and accurate lessons that middle school and high school social studies teachers won't have to debunk. And it's highly engaging because the connections to other topics and subject areas will never end. We have both been teaching for over ten years, but those three years felt different—more meaningful.

Teaching these kinds of lessons felt good. It felt right. And we were thrilled to learn that—not only from our standpoint as teachers, but for students and parents as well—social studies, when done properly, could change our students' lives.

———————

In this book, we have stories to share, ideas for you to implement, and actionable items to help with not only the transition to teaching social studies, but changing the way you think about primary instruction in general. You might begin to notice things in your teaching that you hadn't before. You might begin to feel differently about your classroom library and the characters that are represented in it. You might feel the need to assume the role of a student/researcher and teach yourself some new information so that you can share it with your students.

Social studies has lots of subtopics that fall under its umbrella. Throughout this book, you'll get an in-depth look at exactly how we've come to incorporate history, sociology, economics, geography, and civics into our primary classrooms. We will discuss practical ways to include these five topics and provide examples that we used in our classrooms. We will discuss how we implemented effective cultural studies that go beyond things like "bring in a cultural dish to share." We will discuss how we can take our reading, writing, STEM, and even PE lessons and put a global spin on them. We understand that there are a lot of things that are difficult for many teachers to talk about in their classrooms, so this book also provides a troubleshooting guide of sorts.

We are grateful to have you along for this journey into making elementary social studies truly important and providing lessons to our students that have a global impact.

CHAPTER ONE

RECOGNIZING AND CELEBRATING CULTURE IN THE CLASSROOM

Revamping social studies in our classrooms, especially creating a huge focus on appreciating culture, was the shift we never knew we needed. We called it our love letter to students. We set out to heal, enlighten, and promote curiosity about our world, and that's exactly what we did.

We taught our first self-created social studies lesson in January of 2017. We were building the car as we drove it down the road. When we first began this work, we found that almost every month of our traditional school year had a nationally recognized heritage month assigned to it: February is Black History Month, March is Women's History Month and Irish American Heritage Month, May is Asian and Pacific American Heritage Month, October is Italian American Heritage Month . . . The list goes on and on. This was a great starting point to help us map out what studying culture in the classroom could look like. However, we do not subscribe to the idea that certain cultures should exclusively be covered during a particular month. This is an example of what we meant when we said that our learning is always evolving. At first, celebrating a culture during its month sounded great. We quickly

realized why that isn't the best idea—that's just where our thinking was years ago when we began this work. We now believe in creating a learning environment where a variety of cultures are always recognized and celebrated year-round.

Working across the country from each other, we began to build monthly social studies units for classes of students in kindergarten through third grade. We knew that once we had piloted these ideas in our own classrooms, we were going to share them with everyone else.

We were initially worried that our students would be terribly bored learning about history and culture, but we quickly realized that it actually brought them to life. They craved learning about real people from real places dealing with real things. Students who were usually reluctant to join in on a conversation suddenly had so much to say, ideas to share, and questions to ask. When we taught about the contributions and struggles of Irish American men and women, our kindergarten students were shocked to learn about the discrimination they faced, and the kids had many opinions about what they would have done in their shoes.

Topics covered when we taught culture during a month
vs. incorporating these topics year-round

As each new month approached, we searched high and low for new stories to tell, a culture to highlight, a rarely considered perspective to present, and a different part of the map to explore. We wanted to make sure we weren't just giving our kids more pumpkins (eventually we *did* create a pumpkin unit, but more about that later).

When the time came for us to dive into Native American Heritage Month, our students were surprised to discover a number of things: First, after watching a series of interviews online, we learned that not all Indigenous people feel that they should be called Indians. The videos explained that Columbus called the First Nations people that he encountered "Indians" because he thought he had crossed the Indian Ocean. Some students were even surprised that there are still Native Americans living today. Students expressed that the only time they ever saw Indigenous people was in the past, typically in images where they were contributing to Thanksgiving dinner with the Pilgrims or fighting cowboys. In fact, they were surprised to learn that there are millions of Indigenous people in the US today. We spent some time in disbelief at this, but then we had to consider that when children aren't exposed to various cultures or people and they are left to fill in the gaps—through books, television, or other forms of media where representation is often nonexistent or stereotypical—it's not surprising that misconceptions like this arise. We listened as Indigenous people shared feelings about some of those hurtful stereotypes circulating about Native Americans. We taught our students that all Native tribes or nations are not exactly the same. They are unique and can have their own customs, traditions, languages, and more.

We also learned about a woman named Naomi Lang. She was the first Native American woman to compete in any Winter Olympics Games. She is an ice skater and also a member of the Karuk tribe, one of the largest tribes in California. We found some videos of her competing in the Winter Olympics on YouTube, and our kindergarten and first grade students were mesmerized. Some were introduced to ice dancing and skating for the first time, which gave them a new idea about what they could be when they grew up.

When they learned about how children in South Korea honor their parents for Parents' Day, our students quickly made the connection between Parents' Day and Mother's Day and Father's Day in the United States. They made a connection to a country on the other side of the world. "Where is South Korea?" "Can we take a field trip there?" "Can we drive there?" "What do they eat there?" "Do they speak Chinese there?" The questions, conversations, and misconceptions that consistently came up during our lessons all amounted to the same things: student engagement and authentic learning.

Students were intrigued and begged to know more. We were often late to lunch because we were taking a "trip" via Google Maps to the country we were learning about that day, looking up a question about a culture that we didn't know the answer to, or sharing our comments about a new topic. Our kindergarten and first grade students had debates and discussions; they shared and defended their opinions while respectfully listening to others.

These culture lessons also provided a chance to learn about some amazing and notable people. When we studied Irish American heritage, we learned about the Sullivan brothers, five brothers who all lost their lives in battle, leading to the Sole Survivor policy. We cleared up the misconception that Alexander Bell invented the telephone, which persists even though in 2002 Congress recognized Antonio Meucci as the actual inventor. Meucci was a poor Italian immigrant who reportedly lacked the twenty dollars that he needed to secure the patent. Meucci even took Bell to court, but he would never gain his due credit.

We also learned about a man named Ettore Boiardi (you might know him as Chef Boyardee) who came to the United States through Ellis Island. He worked in a kitchen but eventually was involved in catering the wedding of a United States president. As we read and talked about him, students noticed the changing of his last name. "Why did he change the way he writes his name? It looks different," a student remarked. We had a lot of conversations about cultural erasure and assimilation, and we talked about how a lot of people were forced (and some actually chose) to have their names simplified in order to blend in. A student commented, "We should send a text message to Ettore Boiardi and tell him to spell his name correctly because we could learn how to say it right!" We love the hearts of young children.

The two of us teachers would talk each night in awe of the connections our students had made and the conversations we were able to facilitate. We were seeing that not only can little kids have big conversations, they have important ideas to contribute and the power to use those mindsets to change the world. We still firmly believe that.

LaNesha

It was February, and we had just completed our Black History unit. In my class, we do tons of heavy learning during Black History Month. I'm talking history, culture, celebrating notable figures—the works!

The area that I teach in has many different cultural backgrounds represented. As we were wrapping up the unit, our room covered in beautiful Black history images, one of my Latina students walked over to me and said, "Mrs. Tabb, this was AWESOME! When are we going to learn about my culture?" Gulp. At that point, it honestly had not occurred to me to explicitly teach any other cultures.

Growing up, we rarely studied culture, and if we did, it was typically during Black History Month. I replayed her words in my head for the next few days. I decided to do a little research—because if I was going to highlight another culture with the same energy that I had just given in February, I would need to learn more. I hopped online to Pinterest, blogs, and websites where teachers can purchase resources created by other teachers. On one site, I typed in "Black history" and filtered the results to only show resources for kindergarten through second grade. I found roughly ten thousand results—and I was pretty satisfied with that number.

I got a little more curious and swapped out Black history for Hispanic and Latinx history. Now there were only about two hundred and thirty results to pick from, and most of them were along the lines of "Cinco de Mayo bingo." That certainly wasn't going to work if I truly wanted to provide my students with an authentic experience. I kept going. Asian American heritage ... down to fifty-four results. Native American heritage: thirty-nine units, and most of those centered around things like "Build a teepee STEM challenge." That's when it hit me. Something needed to be done.

When the next school year came around, we had many conversations about what a kickoff to social studies for August would look like. The first thing we wanted to do to was make sure that our students had a solid understanding of our social studies subtopics. We created anchor charts with plenty of photo support so that students would be able to connect with each topic. As we taught lessons throughout the rest of the year, we could refer to these anchor charts.

After our students had an understanding of social studies, we considered what they would need to know before they dived into cultures and places that they may not have heard about. We decided that we would use August to get them excited about celebrating and understanding other peoples' cultures by connecting them to their own. We wanted to give them an overview about what they were going to be lucky enough to study for the year.

Let's Unpack

"Where I'm from in Iraq, boys and girls go to different schools. When I came here, it was really strange for me to sit next to a boy." One of Naomi's fourth grade students shared this with her peers in a small gifted-and-talented pull-out group.

In her seventh year of teaching, Naomi knew better and was doing better, like the great Maya Angelou inspired her to. She knew that instead of finding out all of her students' favorite animals, asking what they wanted to be when they grew up, or doing a simple but fun icebreaker activity to get the scoop on her new group of kids, it was much more important to get to know them culturally.

Had Naomi not inquired about her students' cultures on the first day with the group, the girl may not have ever felt comfortable sharing this observation. Naomi's thankful that she did, because it enabled both her and the student to remain cognizant of this fact throughout the remainder of the school year. The pull-out group consisted of four boys and five girls. How might Naomi have interpreted the student's apprehension at sitting next to a boy or even being partnered up with one if she didn't know her culturally? She might have assumed the girl was simply being defiant when in reality she was uncomfortable.

Learning to intentionally seek to understand our students on a cultural level was the turning point in our ability to build stronger relationships with them and their parents too. During our first years of teaching, building strong relationships with our students was always the goal. It's what they teach us in school, it's what they stress in professional-development sessions, and it's a recognized, well-known practice among all of us teachers who strive to be highly effective. But when we look back now, we cringe at the superficial and surface-level methods we used to get to know our students. Sure, we did get to know them, but we often think about how we could have known them better or known them differently. What pitfalls, behavior issues, or academic roadblocks could we have avoided if we had valued recognizing and celebrating culture in the classroom the way that we do now?

A failure to examine the biases we may have had also held us back from getting to know our students well. Implicit biases are the subconscious attitudes and beliefs that we all hold. There's no question of *if* any of us have biases, but rather what they are, who they are directed toward, and how often they play a role in the way we treat and educate our students. Other educators can probably relate when we share that in our first few years of teaching we were bright-eyed, bushy-tailed, and excited to change lives, while also clinging to our curriculums and reading programs for dear life like a ship's captain relying on a lighthouse to keep her from crashing and ruining everything. We had the best intentions and were striving to teach everyone, but we overlooked a key practice: acknowledging our biases and the ways our teaching was based only in our own cultural knowledge. Simultaneously, we were failing to intentionally acknowledge, appreciate, and integrate the many fascinating, different, and complex cultures that our students brought into the classroom with them daily.

When we say culture here, we are not only referring to students' ethnicities, races, and languages but also to the way things are done in their communities, socials groups, and homes. Our students do not leave their own cultures at the classroom door, and they should not suddenly be forced to navigate their teacher's or school's culture because we (knowingly or unknowingly) deem it the most important in the room.

Once, Naomi noticed a third grade student who didn't seem like himself. He had gotten in trouble in class and was out in the hallway. He was former student of hers, so she struck up a conversation with him. Turns out that since it was Ramadan, he had been fasting (for the first time in his life). So, what his teacher mistook for a bad attitude was really just a "hangry" child whose actions needed to be contextualized with his culture. Experiences like that make us wonder how many issues we have had with students that were based in culture and not behavior, as we'd assumed.

Getting to know our classes on a cultural level was one of the best moves we've ever made as teachers. Knowing that a student's favorite colors are red, green, and black is one thing, but it is another to discover that red, green, and black are colors that bring him a sense of pride because his father is from Kenya and those colors each have a special meaning culturally. Getting to know a student that way allows you to truly build a strong relationship. To this particular student, who was so proud of his Kenyan heritage, a teacher choosing to use the book *For You Are a Kenyan Child* by Kelly Cunnane for a read-aloud meant the world, and it became more meaningful to his classmates because they had a connection to Kenya in the room.

Naomi

As a student who went through the American school system but had parents born in the small developing country of Antigua, I know it would have meant the world to me to have a book, lesson, or even a location shout-out on a map from a single teacher in K–12. I don't even know that a single teacher of mine was even aware that my parents immigrated to this country. Not a single one asked. Not a single lesson led me to say, "Hey! That's where my family is from!" Instead, I wanted to be seen as American. I didn't want anyone to know where my parents came from, that they ate goat meat, listened to soca and calypso music, and had a huge carnival where they danced, colorfully clothed, in the streets every year from dusk until dawn. What an impact my teacher knowing about this huge part of me and getting to celebrate with my classmates would have had on me. If I could see that my teachers valued diverse cultures, I would have been more inclined to share about my own.

Don't Fear Culture

When we take the time to recognize and celebrate the differences and similarities in our students' cultures, we give them the opportunity to see the connection between themselves and others around the globe. In kindergarten and first grade, by nature of their ages, kids are brutally honest. This is a great thing! We can give them the language to use when interacting with people who are different from them. Let them share their thoughts. Teach them to have respectful discourse with their peers.

We have had conversations with so many teachers who are afraid to jump into cultural topics because they fear that their students will be closed-minded due to things they may have heard at home or say something that the teacher won't have an immediate answer for. That's okay! Kids are at school to learn. There is always the possibility you are exposing them to something that they heard the opposite of at home.

We have come to believe that a curiosity about other cultures is best rooted in a firm knowledge of one's own cultural background. That means considering our experiences with our own culture and understanding how important our foods, holidays, religions, etc. are to us. Then we can begin to grasp and respect how important other peoples' cultures are to them. To implement this with our students, we do lots of cultural activities.

At the start of each year, we have our students complete culture flip-books or culture "cases." The culture case and the flip-book both contain similar content. One is more primary friendly, but in both of these activities, we ask students to take the case or flip-book home and discuss the best way to share things that are important to them culturally. They are asked to define culture in their own words, share about their clothing, food, celebrations, language, and more. In some of our other exercises, we ask students to get even more specific when discussing culture. For example, instead of simply sharing the kind of foods they eat, we might ask a student to share *how* they eat it, *where* they eat it, what utensils are necessary, and so forth. Students are asked to explore the idea that they can belong to multiple cultural groups. Every part of our lives is tied to culture, and cultural associations can be national, ethnic, linguistic, religious, related to gender, class, place—literally everything. These activities help us to truly know our students, and they give us insight into our students' experiences. We invite students to share aspects of their lives like clothing styles, celebrations, dances, languages, art—you name it! Of course, during the first few weeks of school we also learn rules and procedures, eat lunch, and play at recess, but we also put in the work to get to know our students on a cultural level.

"Why does your mom wear that 'scarf'?"

When we've talked to other educators about implementing this practice in their rooms, sometimes their response is that their class is all white and there isn't any culture to discover. But just because your class is all white doesn't automatically mean all your students have the same traditions, languages, celebrations, religions, or beliefs. We'll give you an example. One educator reached out to us and asked if we really thought she needed to do the culture case if her class was all white. We told her to go ahead and send it home, just to see what happened. As her students took turns sharing their cultures, an interesting conversation ensued:

Student A: "So on Sundays, my family always goes to a park that is near my grandma's house. We play and have dinner there."

Student B: "Oh, cool. That's after you get out of church?"

Student A: "Church?"

Student B: "Yeah, of course. It's Sunday, so you have to go to church."

What a critical conversation began there! A student was convinced that everyone went to church on Sunday just because their own family did. But consider the impact of the conversation: the student's assumption that "of course you go to church on Sunday" gives us insight into how we can live our lives thinking that everyone is or should be just like us—and if they aren't, then they are weird or different. When we aren't willing to deal with weird or different, our biases are born. And we all know what unchecked biases can turn into. But because this teacher took a leap of faith and tried the culture case activity, she was able to allow her students to bear witness to a real-life illustration of the notion that not all people are like you, and that's more than alright.

Unpacking our cultures is complicated. Especially for students who aren't exactly sure what culture is. We like to give our students many personal examples and enlist help from adults or older siblings at home to help them understand different aspects of their culture. The conversation during our culture work time buzzes with authenticity and real connection. Students are either amazed to have a cultural connection with a another student or in awe of something they just learned about a fellow classmate. Two of our students were delightfully surprised to discover that another student in class also celebrated Eid and Ramadan, even though she didn't wear a hijab like they did.

These activities also created bonds between kids who realized their families shared the same language or simply spoke a language other than English at home, even if it wasn't the same as theirs. For us, as teachers, learning about the languages spoken at home made it easy for us to better communicate with parents. We were able to use the information we learned to send class newsletters and other communications to parents in their home languages. To achieve this, we used Google Translate. The translations weren't always perfect, so it was important to make the parents aware of the method used to create them. This allowed us to let the parents know that even if they found any errors that might have resulted from a poor translation, we meant no disrespect to them or their language. The most important thing was to give parents and guardians access to the information that was shared.

Culture is worth celebrating, and celebrating it in the classroom helps students feel seen. We always take the time to let our students proudly present their culture cases or flipbooks to the class. There are a few things we teach before presentations. Students learn to:

- Celebrate differences.
- Give compliments.
- Ask appropriate and respectful questions.
- Be proud of the unique aspects of their own cultures and the cultures of others.
- Never use the word "weird" when what they really mean is different.
- Be respectful of things because it's something they haven't experienced yet.

Create a Culture Corner

Naomi

One year, I had a first grade student—I'll call him Kyle—from Bulgaria. He had come to class in December only speaking Bulgarian, and I had taught the rest of the class three to four Bulgarian words a week so we could communicate with him. Kyle loved when our class learned a few phrases so we could communicate with him. In just six short months, he gained a great command of the English language.

But in the time between kindergarten and first grade (I looped with my class), Kyle seemed to lose the sense of pride he had once had in his first language. His parents told me they were hoping to bring him back to visit their home country the following summer because he had started refusing to speak Bulgarian at home. He wanted to only speak English. He told me he was forgetting Bulgarian, but he was also becoming more and more ashamed of his home language as he continued to be immersed in all things American. When Kyle's parents told me he wouldn't even speak Bulgarian at home, I made it my mission to impress upon the entire class once again how beautiful, unique, and amazing each of our cultures are. I made sure that they knew that our cultures are something to talk about!

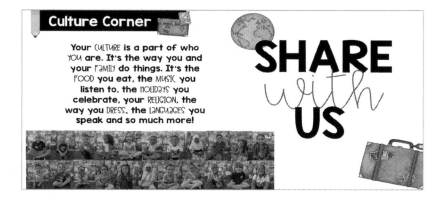

Culture Corner

Your CULTURE is a part of who YOU are. It's the way you and your FAMILY do things. It's the FOOD you eat, the MUSIC you listen to, the HOLIDAYS you celebrate, your RELIGION, the way you DRESS, the LANGUAGES you speak and so much more!

SHARE with US

Want to get your students ridiculously excited about culture? Get ridiculously excited about culture yourself! This is how, halfway through the school year, Naomi's classroom's Wednesday afternoon Culture Corner was born. Each Wednesday, students had fifteen minutes to show or teach something from their culture or home life against the backdrop of a slide Naomi had created. When we tell you these kids looked forward to Culture Corner, we mean that *every* Monday *and Tuesday* morning they asked, "Is it Wednesday yet?" It was not their first time talking about culture, so the students knew what Naomi meant when she said they'd be sharing parts of their culture with each other.

At the first Culture Corner, Naomi shared that her family listened to calypso music, and she played a song. The student teacher shared that she had become fluent in American Sign Language because her mother was deaf, and she taught the students a few signs. Then Naomi turned it over to the kids. She told them that they could share something—*any-thing*—from their culture or home life.

When she saw that Kyle had his hand up to volunteer to share next, Naomi immediately called on him. He went up in front of the entire class and proudly taught them all how to say some funny phrases in Bulgarian. When his friends told him how cool Bulgarian was and applauded his home language, Kyle's smile was priceless. Naomi told him she wished she knew more than one language and expressed how proud she was of him for being bilingual.

Next, another student counted to twenty in Vietnamese as the class repeated after him. One week, two students presented together to teach about why they wear hijabs in school. Another described how his family celebrated Christmas, and one brave student even showed everyone some amazing dance moves!

Each Wednesday, for fifteen minutes starting at one o'clock, Naomi made time for about three students to show or tell about something from their culture and then receive compliments or answer questions about it. We definitely recommend implementing something similar in your classroom if you can make the time for it. Fifteen minutes once a week made a world of difference in our classes. Here are some of the prompts we use:

1. Do you speak any other languages? Students can teach other students how to say different words in their home language.
2. What is a holiday celebrated in your culture? Tell us all about it.
3. Which celebration from your culture is your favorite?

4. How does your family celebrate birthdays? If they don't, can you tell us why?

5. What is your favorite food from your culture? What's in it? How do you make it? When do you make it?

6. What music does your family listen to? (If possible, play a song for the class.)

7. Show us some dance moves from your culture.

8. Tell us or show us what people in your culture wear and why.

9. Teach us about a game from your culture.

After each presentation, students are encouraged to comment, compliment, or ask a question. This follow-up really encourages more students to want to share. As teachers, we always wave our own hands around wildly and impatiently waiting to be called on so that we can compliment whatever each child chooses to share. They love this! They feel seen, they feel heard, and they receive the message week after week that their culture and the cultures of their peers is unique and something to be proud of.

As teachers, we must always be aware of the great amount of influence we hold with our students. We're being watched by our students just as much when we praise one student's culture as when we don't use the same level of enthusiasm, praise, or engagement for another. We must always take care not to stereotype students or create the illusion that all students with the same culture or background do the exact same things the exact same way.

Stereotypes can be harmful. In October of 2018 we saw some educators in Idaho dressed up as stereotypes of Mexican people and a border wall meant to keep people from entering the United States. We knew that important lessons in our classrooms were in order. We scrapped the lessons we were originally going to teach and taught our first graders about stereotypes instead. We started out by letting them know that whenever we tell people that we teach first grade, many folks assume that all first graders are nose pickers, unable to read, very loud and messy, wear stinky socks, and are unable to walk in a line properly.

Needless to say, our students were outraged: "But they don't even know us!" "We don't pick our noses!" "Well, not all of us pick our noses!"

We discussed how stereotypes about races, cultures, genders, ages, disabilities, and ethnicities are not fair to the people they were about. They came to the conclusion that it was important to truly get to know people before making assumptions.

Little Kids and Big Conversations

You could be thinking, "You guys have THESE sorts of conversations in kindergarten? My kids could never!" But they can.

Remember how we told you that we believe little kids can do big things? Having a conversation is one of them. But you have to explicitly teach them how to do it. From the first day of school, we are getting our students set up for conversation. In kindergarten, this starts with literally teaching them how to sit on the carpet, speak clearly, make eye contact, listen carefully, and take turns as they talk. We teach them that a conversation takes more than one person and that you have to have some strategies to keep the conversation going.

Kathy Collins is a phenomenal educator, and we were able to watch her teach a group of children that a conversation is a lot like a game you play with a balloon where you hit it back and forth. She told them that when one person says something, it's like they bopped the balloon over to you. If you don't say anything back, then the balloon pops, and the conversation is over. So, you need to be ready to keep the conversation going with a sentence stem / conversation prompt.

We give our students tons of opportunities to practice these skills. Students are asked to talk about something from their first day in our classrooms. It might be a piece of art, a sample of opera music, or a debate on who the best Disney princess is. We think it is important to give them nonacademic topics to talk about before we give them heavier topics. When the topics are nonacademic, the students are able to focus on the art of simply keeping a conversation going. This skill will set them up for having complex conversations about culture—and social studies at large.

Culture matters. Culture is important. It is not enough to hang an "All Are Welcome Here" sign in the hallway or to display flags from around the world on a bulletin board. We must do the work to uncover the important truths about our students that make them the individuals

Some of the slides we use to teach conversation skills

that they are. This work has to be intentional and explicit. When students understand and appreciate their own cultures, they can learn to understand and appreciate the cultures of others. They will be able to find similarities and differences and make connections to citizens around the globe.

UNPACK

Appreciating other cultures begins with understanding our own. Primary students can explore this concept through anchor charts, maps and globes, culture lessons, and conversation prompts.

IMPACT

When we prioritize culture in the classroom, we give students the opportunity to connect with themselves, each other, and the world at large in a meaningful way.

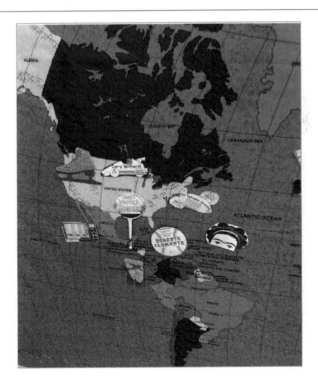

CHAPTER TWO

PROBLEMATIC HISTORY LESSONS

History is furious debate informed
by evidence and reason.
—JAMES W. LOEWEN

History in primary—that's no big deal, right? How much does that really matter?

Let's do a test. Finish the phrase:

In fourteen hundred ninety-two, Columbus

_____.

You said, "Sailed the ocean blue," didn't you? Who among us hasn't recited this little rhyme in perfect unison with our classmates at some point during our elementary school days? You can pretty much walk up to anyone in public and ask them to finish that sentence and they will. Why is that? Because of us—classroom teachers. For decades we have taught students a singular narrative about Columbus. A narrative that is so flawed and debunked that it is embarrassing.

Because Columbus Day was approaching, we were a few days into our Christopher Columbus research (because we had some serious unlearning to do). We were shocked to find that sailing the ocean blue

was the last thing this man should be known for. As we read, we had so many questions. Were our own teachers just unaware of his history? Did they know and still not care to stray from the path of what's always been done? Why does he even have a holiday? Why do we celebrate this man and teach lessons that paint him as a brave hero? Why are we lying to our students year after year and teaching them that he discovered America? We asked ourselves these questions as we uncovered more and more of the horrors that Columbus partook in during his time.

One more question that we asked ourselves was "Why are we just learning this information now when we are in our thirties?" That was the day we decided to tell our kids the truth about Columbus.

We will admit that during our first few years of teaching, we had done the Columbus crafts and sang the Columbus rhyme with our students, just like teachers had with us when we were in school. We can only hope that a future teacher of our early students was able to tell them the truth that we didn't. We regret the impact we may have had on those groups of students in that particular area.

We also want to acknowledge that since we live in a society where most of our founders believed in white supremacy, it is impossible to ever accurately and fully teach a lesson that hasn't been impacted by white supremacy in some form. While we are aware of its ever-looming presence and impact, we try to ensure that it is not the focus of every single lesson we teach.

Perhaps you've heard the claim that history in the American school system has been whitewashed. When we say that, we mean that the stories of events and people that we learn about are created with a bias to portray white men and some white women as brave explorers and pioneers. White people are presented as the first to accomplish some great feat, having invented something that changed the world forever, or single-handedly making America what it is today. Sure, they enslaved Black men and women, killed countless numbers of Indigenous people, and are still living on stolen land, but with whitewashing, these horrific acts and practices are explained away as "just the way things were," examples of Manifest Destiny, or the necessary means to an end that happened so long ago with so little connection to the present that we should just forget about them. We love the quote from Lin-Manuel Miranda that says, "History is entirely created by the person who tells the story." History is tricky because none of us were there! We are left putting together the pieces that are available to us or searching for perspectives that have intentionally been left out. This could be one of the reasons for the oversimplification of history lessons in school. Because of the way many history textbooks and lessons are written, nonwhite voices and perspectives are left out, erased, or revised to fit a narrative that white America is more comfortable with. An example is the narrative that aims for us to be completely in love with George Washington despite the fact that he owned 317 people at the time of his death, including over 140 children. Our history lessons often don't include information like this. No, we pretend that the heroes of the past were all hero and nothing more. Owning people is wrong. It is wrong now, and it was wrong then. The reality is that the people of the past were flawed humans—not all good and many with some bad mixed in. They were whole human beings who were imperfect, and a lot of times, downright awful. We skip over these truths and simply tell our students the feel-good stories, but we owe them the truth and the full picture.

Now, instead of celebrating Columbus Day with craft projects about boats, we teach our students the truth about the events surrounding Columbus. We let them know what we learned when we were their age, and then present them with the facts. We then have a debate about whether or not he should be celebrated, and we discuss our reasons to support our beliefs as a class. In Denver, where Naomi lived, Indigenous Peoples' Day was actually celebrated in lieu of Columbus Day. We brought this into the conversation with our students. Not only did our classes learn the truth about Columbus and the (age-appropriate) details of his early explorations to the "New World," we got into another debate about who should be celebrated on this day and why.

Most teachers are required to cover a holiday like this. We think that's great, actually. It gives us the opportunity to tell our students how this content is traditionally taught and then ask them to weigh that out against the facts we research and present. A class debate on whether or not cities should celebrate Indigenous Peoples' Day instead of Columbus Day grows critical-thinking skills. Some students will even ask to take civil action. They might want to know why some places changed the holiday but the place where they live didn't. This is an example of the kind of engagement we are always after. Real. Organic. Authentic. This kind of thinking carries. It carries much further than reciting the "ocean blue" rhyme for the one hundredth time in pre-K and then again in kindergarten and then again in first grade and then again in . . . you know where this is going.

Hopefully, you are starting to see how much of a big deal history in primary classrooms is. When we teach lessons in kindergarten, we are planting seeds. Because our history narratives are largely centered around the positive contributions of white males, the seeds we plant with years of glowing lessons about Washington,

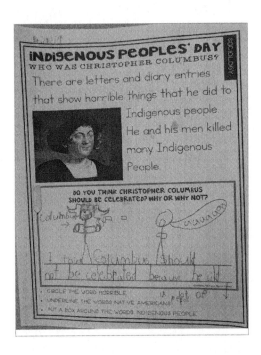

Lincoln, Bell, Lee, Franklin, and all the rest of them, will grow into biases. These biases are a result of our impact as teachers—they come from the fact that students are hit over the head with lessons of the great things these men did, as if no one else was a factor in making this country, this world, what it is today.

These whitewashed narratives make some students sit up a little taller in class. "Everyone that has done anything great that my teacher told me about looks JUST like me!" Those same students have been and will continue to be affirmed in their daily lives—by the majority of children's literature they read, television characters they see, and often, the communities they live in where everyone looks like them. They may grow up to proclaim that there's no such thing as discrimination or racism, or they will scoff at the need for Black History Month or historically Black colleges and universities. And why wouldn't they? When your culture is dominant, accepted, centered, and held up as the standard, seeing someone else centered *would* be off-putting. It's why we see such a visceral reaction to a little girl in a shirt that says "Black Girl Magic" and why "all lives matter" is an immediate response to someone saying that Black lives shouldn't be disposable. History lessons are a big deal. We plant these narratives early on, and they become biases, which eventually become our beliefs. The impact of getting this wrong is monumental.

As we mentioned before, the heritage feature for most months helped us plan how to introduce our students to historical figures and events that we'd use to teach them about underrepresented stories, cultures, and history from around the globe. The heritage framework provided a good starting point for our research, and as we proceeded, we realized that there were so many truths we'd been robbed of ourselves. "Why are we just learning this now?" we constantly asked ourselves. "Why did we learn the same stories, learn about the same people, and learn the same lies from kindergarten through twelfth grade?" It's no wonder we and many of our colleagues are stuck teaching false narratives. It's what is readily available in our reading and social studies programs, and it's what we were taught and accepted as truth for our entire lives.

Largely because we recognize our own miseducation, our social studies lessons end with us encouraging students to go home and teach others what they have just learned. "Guess what? If your parents went to school in the United States, they probably don't know this, because they were probably taught the same information that I was," we always say. "Your job is to go home and teach them the truth!" It always gets students excited to think that they possibly know something their parents don't.

Cinco de Mayo

When Cinco de Mayo was approaching in 2018, we were more than excited to research an accurate historical account of this holiday. We had Mexican families come in and share that they did not enjoy seeing this day reduced to tacos, maracas, and other Mexican stereotypes. We teamed up with our friend Kay Valdez to provide the truth for students. Kay is a primary teacher who is passionate about equitable education that meets the needs of all learners.

There's something thrilling about empowering students with the truth. Giving them information and equipping them with the facts they need to make informed decisions about the world around them is one of our favorite things to do. As Cinco de Mayo approached, we made sure to create a resource for our students, as well as others, that would help them discuss the stereotypes and misconceptions surrounding this day. When we taught the lesson to our students, they were captivated by the Battle of Puebla, which took place in

1862. That content alone made for a great lesson, but we took things a step further to talk to our students about how some people have expressed hurt over the way this day has been celebrated insensitively, even though they may have good intentions. We let students weigh in on the importance of this day and the stereotypes often associated with it. A quick Google search for Cinco de Mayo immediately resulted in images of only maracas, tacos, sugar skulls, and piñatas. Our students had just learned the history of Cinco de Mayo, so they were a little confused about why there weren't any pictures of battles, parades, or people from Puebla, Mexico, honoring this day.

Social studies made teaching fun again. Researching and teaching these lessons to our students was as informative and exciting for us as it was for them. Learning about a story, presenting the facts to our classes, and then asking their opinions became the routine. They couldn't wait to find out who or what we'd be learning about next. Other educators that we shared our lessons with had the same thing to say. We excitedly shared our stories on social media and our blogs and got feedback from across the country. Even teachers in Canada and Australia were contacting us. They couldn't believe how quickly social studies became their favorite subject to teach!

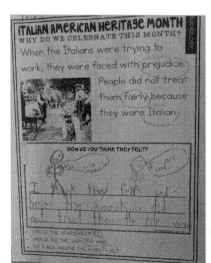 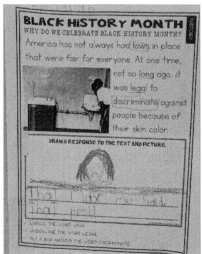

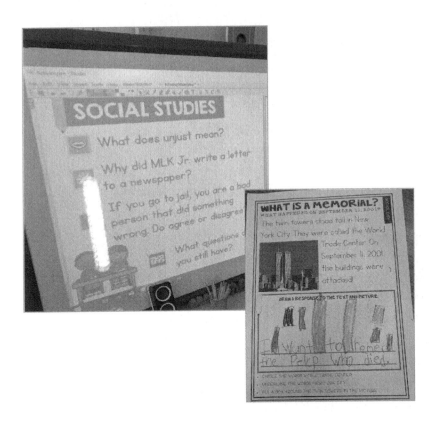

Thanksgiving

Let's talk about Thanksgiving in the primary classroom. Oh yes, we are going there. Every year in November, teachers gear up to educate their students about the first Thanksgiving. This time in history is often painted as a day back in 1621 that brought the Wampanoag people and Pilgrims together for a nice dinner. Some quick research will tell you that that story is flawed. The truth is, it wasn't even the first Thanksgiving.

Was there a feast? Sure! The feast of 1621 happened, but not for the reasons we think. Also, events like these happened all the time. A day of thanks with a feast was a very normal practice. Thanksgiving wouldn't even be recognized as a national holiday until the 1860s—nearly two hundred years later. So why are we still telling children that the feast of 1621 was the first Thanksgiving? Is it because, once again, we've painted a safe and pretty picture, this time of the nice "Indians" showing the poor Pilgrims how to plant food? There is historical evidence to suggest that the Pilgrims didn't even invite the Native people to join them at first; it's possible they only felt compelled to after the Natives heard gunfire and came to see what was happening.

We tell the story of Squanto "the friendly Indian" (that title in itself suggests that the rest of the Indians were not friendly). Tisquantum (Squanto's real name) had a tragic history of being enslaved, sold, and escaping cleverly, but his story has been reduced to "the guy that helped Pilgrims grow food." Some teachers even dress their students up to re-create this meal and talk about the friendships that formed on that fateful day. We go down to the construction paper closet and use up all the brown paper to make "Indian vests and headdresses" and create an "Indian name" to be called for the day. The other half of the classroom has to dress up as Pilgrims so they can sit and have a school lunch because it's cute.

We like cute as much as the next teacher, but friends, there is a time to be cute and then there's a time to be truthful. The truth is important. Appropriating sacred cultural clothing to be cute is wrong and insensitive. We must always consider missing perspectives and how children might be harmed when we don't have the full picture. The fourth Thursday in November is a far cry from cutesy for many in the United States.

For some it is the National Day of Mourning, a yearly protest that has occurred annually since 1970. This day is intended to serve as a reminder of the mistreatment and murder of hundreds of their Native ancestors, as well as the acknowledgment of the struggles and fights many Native men, women, and children are still facing today. Depending on the grade level you work with, how you choose to deliver this information will vary. With the kindergarteners and first graders we teach, we talk about Indigenous people being treated unfairly and being hurt. You can give more details about this treatment to an older group of students.

As the day approached, we began to brainstorm how we could educate our students about Thanksgiving and teach it accurately. We wanted facts, and we sought to tell an untold story. We aren't historians, but we do know how to research. We did some digging and some synthesizing to bring this information to our students. We pored over texts and articles. We sent each other messages back and forth for weeks every time we uncovered more about Thanksgiving, especially when we learned about the "mother of Thanksgiving," Sarah Josepha Hale.

We learned that this woman went on a thirty-something-year campaign starting in the 1830s to make Thanksgiving a national holiday. Think about that for just a minute: over thirty years of writing letter after letter. She wrote letters to four different US presidents asking for Thanksgiving to be made into a holiday. She was also a widow who had to work to earn a living for her children. She ended up becoming the editor in chief of the most widely read ladies' magazine of that time. She used that magazine, *Godey's Lady's Book*, to publish more letters, articles, and narratives about the benefits of making Thanksgiving a holiday.

These articles were used to sway the minds of ladies with stories of families that were torn apart but unable to reconcile by having a dinner together. The idea spread. But her proposed holiday was rejected for decades until Abraham Lincoln took office and the Civil War was about to break out. Finally, in 1863, Thanksgiving was made into a national holiday.

During the thirty years she'd been working on the project, she also used her magazine to publish something very critical to Thanksgiving: recipes. Recipes for foods like turkey, dressing, cranberry sauce, and pumpkin pie. The same foods that grace some of our Thanksgiving menus to this very day.

Sarah Hale is largely responsible for the cases of cranberries stacked in a pile taller than you at the market in November. Have you ever stopped to think about why so many people make similar dishes on Thanksgiving? A fun way to kick off a discussion about this in school is by asking students what they are going to be having for dinner on

Thanksgiving if they celebrate. Once everyone's lists are compiled and we realize they're very similar, we jokingly ask: "Oh my gosh, did all of your families call each other and plan to make the same things?" After a chuckle, it's a great segue into teaching a more accurate history of how Thanksgiving became a holiday.

And what of that feast in 1621? Why do we think of that as the first Thanksgiving? That's actually Sarah's doing too. Remember, this feast happened two hundred years prior to the establishment of the holiday. Sarah was said to have loved this imagery. In her opinion, even though it was inaccurate, it was the perfect symbol for coming together to share a meal. Her magazine started to run illustrations of this feast depicting the Natives and Pilgrims joining together to have turkey pie. After a while, the narrative stuck. It clearly had an impact on people, because the story and imagery have been passed down to this day.

James Loewen defines history as "furious debate informed by evidence and reason." For us, that means that no one can ever be completely sure of anything. Even with firsthand accounts, you have to remember that every event or series of events involved multiple parties. Not all of those stories were told. Some were intentionally skewed or covered up. There's always another fact to find or misconception to debunk. We even tell our students this! It's important for them to understand that this is what we know *now*. We teach our students that a historian (even a young one) is always looking for more information! Historical events can be told from an infinite amount of perspectives, and it's important for students to understand this.

This is tragic to us because history, when taught properly, is beyond fascinating. However, if you ask people what their least favorite subject was in school, many cringe at the thought of history classes. We teachers really messed that up. History is thrilling. It's tragic. It's basically a roadmap for things that we see happening now. Changing the way it's taught is one of the biggest reasons why we wanted to write this book. We want to get teachers, schools, and districts fired up and passionate about the truth.

One teacher told us that she wasn't even allowed to read a book to her class about the life of Dr. Martin Luther King Jr. In an email, the teacher was told by the principal that that was not a topic to be taught. We're always so curious about this—this notion that knowing the truth will be so detrimental that we must do everything we can to hide it. What's the worst that could happen if we teach that in addition to being the first president, George Washington also enslaved a lot of people? Would it be that students learn that our nation's history is flawed, with devastating ripple effects that affect us even today? That we learn how to take difficult information and process it and have critical conversations about it? We gain perspective or empathy? We learn to do better and learn from mistakes from the past? What is the worst that could truly happen?

You might work at a school where the worst that could happen is that you'll get fired. There might be things you can do before that happens. Maybe you can request a meeting with your administrators and advocate for accurate history lessons and their benefits or your staff can meet for professional development about how to teach about racism so that the entire school can work on things together. It's possible that you can take steps to get the ball rolling without putting your job in jeopardy.

This line of thinking is something that we hope all teachers are empowered to follow. You don't have to wait for accurate history lessons to be made for you. It may take some extra work, but you can build your own lessons and put them in front of your students. We all have so much information at our fingertips. Don't worry, we will discuss this in more detail later in this book.

Black History

When you think about Black History Month in any grade level, but specifically at the primary level, who do you think is being talked about? It always seems to be the same key players: Dr. Martin Luther King Jr., Rosa Parks, Jackie Robinson, Harriet Tubman, and Ruby Bridges. On a walk down most K–2 hallways in any school in America during February, you're likely to find either nothing—because the teachers are too uncomfortable to "go there" and Black history is swept under the rug—or "I have a dream" writing prompts, MLK Jr. coloring sheets, and a craft project with a smiling Rosa Parks glued onto a little yellow bus.

We see these "history" projects in our school buildings and plastered all over the internet. We know they are out there. They are being used in place of real lessons that really matter and could have a lasting impact on the students who so badly need them. Any time an educator asks, "Do you have anything cute for Black History Month?" it's problematic. It's not cute. Some things are too critical for crafts. Our classrooms may be the only places that our students get these lessons or hear the truth. We owe it to them to expose them to a deeper, richer, more colorful, and accurate history.

It is important for our students to know that Martin Luther King Jr. was more than just a dream. He was a great man who led the Civil Rights Movement and also a human man with flaws of his own. He was arrested twenty-nine times and had an extremely low public-approval rating at the time of his death, and yet we've all convinced ourselves that "he would never protest or make a scene if he were here today." We've taken the legacy of a man whose goal was to end racism and discrimination and reduced it to some feel-good sound bites that post well on Instagram. When we humanize the people we introduce our students to, we give them realistic people to look up to. They can see themselves in these people and can truly be inspired to make a difference.

When approaching history topics, specifically Black history in America (which can also just be called American history), there seems to be a pressure to bring lessons to life with acting, role playing, or some interactive component. There are many times when this practice can be amazingly engaging, for example, having students present historical monologues or holding mock elections. Teaching about the enslavement of an entire race of people is not the time to try this out. We see it every year, though. Every year, some teachers think it will be "powerful" to show their students just how bad slavery was by simulating these traumatic and horrible historic events.

They allow white children to watch as they force students who are Black, Indigenous, and people of color (the term BIPOC is sometimes used to identify Black people, Indigenous people, and people of color) to be traumatized and embarrassed in front of their classmates. We must ask ourselves who is served by practices like these. They are usually led by a well-intentioned white teacher who wants his or her white students to really *get it*. BIPOC should not have to show their pain to prove how horrific something truly was or to be seen as worthy of being cared about. This practice is harmful for all students.

We want to say it plainly: it is never okay to ask your students, no matter their race, to do any sort of role playing or reenactment of slavery. No, we don't need students to go through an Underground

Railroad-themed escape room or obstacle course (it happened) in the gym. No, we are not going to ask students to "pretend they are a slave master" and make a poster to catch their runaway slave. These actions are wrong and can be traumatic for students of all backgrounds.

The history of enslavement in America is often glossed over in lessons as if it was just a natural part of the past that holds no connection to the present day. Enslaved people are also constantly referred to as *slaves*—as if that's just who they happened to be. No, they were *enslaved*, they weren't slaves. Words matter. We need to talk about why they were enslaved. Talk about who enslaved them. We can't say, "That's just the way things were a long time ago." It was racist and it was wrong. Label it.

Also, throughout the year—not just in February—we can't forget to focus on more than just the Black struggle. Black people are so much more. Seek out new stories of Black lives and make sure they get told all year long. Something we hate seeing each year on the internet is teachers commenting about how much fun Black History Month was and how much their kids loved learning about all of these people and stories. They go on to say they wish they had time to do more. *Um . . . you can.* In March. And April. And then again in May. You can even teach about Black (American) history from August to December too. Black History is not a Girl Scout Cookie. It can be appreciated and taught year-round.

Over 80 percent of the teachers in America are white. We find ourselves in many conversations online and sometimes in person with white teachers who tell us, "I wish you could teach my class because you're Black." They tell us how uncomfortable they are even using the word *Black* in front of their students. They aren't sure about where to start or what to say, so many of them choose to opt out of addressing Black history in their classrooms, hoping the next teacher will touch on it. But what if they don't?

Many teachers tell us about their good intentions in order to excuse the impact of their surface level or nonexistent lessons on Black history. It's important for us to understand something that has become an important concept for many of us: impact matters more than our intentions. If you tried to make a friend laugh by pulling their chair out from underneath them, but the impact was that they fell and broke their arm, surely you wouldn't spend your time trying to get them to see that harm wasn't your intention. Focusing on your intention instead of the very real and painful harm caused would be selfish. It is something you did out of a need to make yourself feel better about your actions, when you would really need to reflect about your impact and do better moving forward.

Another thought regarding teachers who feel that teaching certain histories makes them uncomfortable: that can't be the reason we skip certain lessons. Multiplying fractions makes Naomi uncomfortable, but if she taught third grade, she'd still have to do it. Telling a Black person you wish they could teach Black history instead of you because it's uncomfortable to you is upsetting for a number of reasons. This tells us you definitely don't discuss Black people at any other time in your classroom, so your students are not exposed to the windows or mirrors (more on those later in Chapter 7) they desperately need. If we, Black women, can teach about white French, British, Spanish, and all sorts of other non-Black explorers and colonizers, then anyone can teach about Black history and people.

If you are uncomfortable, then we challenge you to reflect on why you feel that you can't teach something that is necessary for *all* students to learn. Do some research so you can come from a more informed place, no matter what your skin color is. Familiarize yourself with this content and teach it anyway. Teaching Black history is not always comfortable. It's not supposed to be. A lot of it is awful and painful.

Naomi

I vividly remember teaching about Ruby Bridges to explore the literary theme of bravery with a fourth grade pull-out group that I worked with. Ruby Bridges was the first Black child to desegregate an all-white school in Louisiana in 1960. My students hadn't ever heard of her. We got our Chromebooks out and began researching. The question I posed was "Do you think it took courage for Ruby Bridges to go to William Frantz Elementary School on the very first day and continue going each day after that? Why or why not?" As we compiled and shared our findings, we happened upon a powerful song about Ruby Bridges on Flocabulary.com. One of the lines goes, "Oh, Ruby, when will all this be over? When will everyone be treated the same? Oh, Ruby Bridges changed the course of history. I never knew a little girl could be so brave."

One of my boys said, "Mrs. O'Brien, I feel like I'm about to cry." I could tell he was worried about what his peers might say. He turned his back to us to hide his tears, but I could see that they were already streaming down his cheeks. Another boy chimed in, "I think I'm going to cry too. This isn't fair. And she's still alive . . . that means this didn't happen that long ago. That's so wrong. Does stuff like this still happen?" I couldn't lie. I had to tell them that it does. I had tears in my own eyes and a huge lump in my throat as well. I told them it was okay to feel sad and mad and even to cry, because this was something that could bring out many emotions. At the end of our lesson, my students, who had previously used examples like soldiers, police officers, and daredevils to define bravery, added another example to their list: a six-year-old girl by the name of Ruby who looked racism and injustice in the face and emitted nothing but courage.

It's not any more comfortable or easy for us to have these discussions just because we are Black. Also: having an all-white class isn't an excuse either. One could argue that a group of white students needs lessons in Black history more than any other group. Students who are raised in an environment that supports, nurtures, and affirms their identity and culture for their entire lives need multiple opportunities to gain perspective and empathy regarding other races and cultures. How will they ever get there if we continue to be scared to teach these lessons?

We have a formula of sorts that we follow:

1. Figure out who or what we are teaching.
2. Ask ourselves whose voice is missing from the narrative.
3. Research.
4. Present multiple voices and ask the students to discuss.

One question that helps us with this is: Where was I?

LaNesha can vividly remember the origin of that question. She was sitting in her sixth grade social studies class. They were learning about the Middle Ages—castles, knights, moats, the whole deal. The teacher asked the class to create a family crest. It needed to have meaning, symbols, etc. She recalls being irritated at this lesson because she, as usual, had no connection to it. None. Why would she? No one in these lessons ever looked the way she looked or did things she thought were interesting. She spent the class thinking, "Who cares? WHERE WAS I DURING THIS TIME?"

She used to ask herself that every time she learned about something in history. She'd wonder, If I were alive at that very moment, what would I be doing? Where would I work? Like our students, if what she was learning wasn't relevant to her, she would just check out.

But what if her teachers had introduced her to a Black man who was living at the exact same time as the knights in their castles? What if they taught her about a king like Mansa Musa of Mali, who was the richest man to walk the earth? Might she have connected to this story? Would she have loved to learn about Africa before the transatlantic slave trade? While Europe was being wiped out with the bubonic plague, Mali was thriving. Mansa Musa was so wealthy that he took a caravan larger than anything you could imagine and made a trek to Mecca. He gave away so much gold on this trip that he actually ruined the economy in Egypt by causing inflation. What if just one time our teachers looked at us and thought about a way to connect us to history?

Most people who aren't history buffs think of history as a series of major events. Think back to your history textbooks and the images of the American Revolution, the Civil War, WWI, and WWII. What do you remember about all of these pictures? Perhaps in our studies of WWII, in between learning about food rationing and sock hops, they could have taught us about the Six Triple Eight Division. This was a special division of Black women in the Women's Army Corps who were tasked with the job of sorting through an unfathomable amount of mail. The mail was backed up, which meant that soldiers weren't hearing from home and so morale was low. These women sorted and shipped the mail out, and as a result, thousands of soldiers were able to receive updates about their families. This is a reminder to revisit ideas from multiple perspectives.

Learning about different views on a subject gives students a critical chance to gain two things: perspective and empathy. Yes, teaching us about Mansa Musa and the Six Triple Eight Division would have given us a chance to see people like us in history, and that's amazing because representation matters. But we would argue that it is equally if not more important for children to ask another question: Where were the people who DO NOT look like me in this story? Showing students the contributions, success stories, and victories of BIPOC can disrupt the default.

When we say default, we mean the idea that white culture is the "norm." Accepted and expected. To give an example: one of our gyms used to have huge walls covered in photos of athletic models. One hundred percent of the models were white, because in our society, white is the default. What if you walked into that very same gym the next day and every single white model had been replaced with a person of Asian descent? Or Black? Or Latinx? Heads would turn! People would notice. When your identity and importance is reinforced in every magazine, television show, princess, lunch box, backpack, picture book, AND school history lesson you're exposed to, some disrupting might be necessary.

We have to teach history—the good, the bad, and the ugly. When we teach our students the truth, we know we are pushing them to think critically about the world they live in, to come up with solutions, and to understand how the past informs and has major effects on the present. We have high-level discussions. We love seeing students' compassion for people and hearing their ideas to make the world a better place. Children are natural problem solvers, but if we don't present any part of American history as problematic, they don't get the chance to engage in a debate that our country should be constantly having with all of its citizens: what can we do to be a better country for everyone? We can't just show our students Black struggle and oppression. Yes, these are most definitely important to talk about. They should be discussed each year of school and connected to the present day so that students can grasp the impact and connection between the past and now. But we must show Black highlight reels too.

So how can you get started in your classroom? What lessons do you usually cover that may need a more accurate version of history brought to light? Which stories are told year after year, grade level after grade level, that you can swap out for new ones? We learned about the same few people our entire time in school. We wish we had been exposed to more. If your students are learning about Martin, Harriet, and Rosa in kindergarten, think about whether they absolutely have to be covered in first grade, second, third, and so on.

The difference educators can make collectively is powerful. Problematic history lessons can stop with us. They can stop with you.

UNPACK

Address problematic history lessons by revealing other perspectives that may be less commonly known or taught. Use these occasions to illustrate distinctions between long-held beliefs and facts.

IMPACT

Exposing students to multiple perspectives on historical events allows them to think critically about the world around them and learn to be more compassionate and open-minded.

CHAPTER THREE

SOCIOLOGY: EXPOSING STUDENTS TO MORE

Sometimes it seems like Americans think that the United States and the world are synonymous—that learning about US history and American ways of life are all that our students need in K–12. When you take a look at some state social studies standards, you see a lot of the same progression, and it's largely focused only on America, especially at the primary level.

In elementary school—if a school even happens to feature social studies—the areas of study seem to be pretty similar. They focus on classroom community, the neighborhood students live in, the city and state they live in, the United States, the geography of the world (but not its people), and then maybe some history of ancient civilizations like the Aztecs or the Egyptians.

We are here to tell you that you can and should teach more and teach it earlier! We used to be in the same boat when it came to social studies, and we can tell you personally that once you branch out, you will never go back to teaching just the basics. You love teaching about community helpers? That's good. But what if you covered community helpers in the Bahamas, Hong Kong, or Venezuela? What if you showed

community helpers during real-life events that affected real people around the world, like in Puerto Rico after Hurricane Maria in 2017? The entire world redefined community helpers as essential workers during the COVID-19 pandemic. The heroes that we are all depending on can be found working on sanitation routes and in hospitals, grocery stores, farms, and warehouses. Going forward, a unit about community helpers might be one of the most important units that we can teach, since we have all witnessed firsthand that the world does not operate without community helpers.

Sociology, or the study of human relationships and institutions, has been around since the days of Plato. But we noticed two problems with what was happening in our own school buildings and the schools of educators around the country we were talking to. Not only were students not really getting sociology lessons in their elementary classrooms, but when they were, what they were being taught was often the same lessons about the same people, usually only Americans and Europeans.

For years elementary schools have inexplicably focused on themes like Johnny Appleseed in history class and square dancing in gym class. One look at a K–2 Pinterest board or hallway of classrooms quickly reveals that students are often missing out on the experience of exploring, and therefore relating to, people from different parts of the world on a consistent basis. There also seems to be a lack of vertical alignment. How incredible would it be if content was organized across grade levels to ensure that classes were all working together to prepare students to go deeper and wider with social studies topics? The Civil Rights Era is definitely an important time in history, but does it have to be taught every February from kindergarten to fifth grade? Imagine the knowledge that could be spread if educators from different grade levels worked together and talked about which topics each grade would cover in order to prepare students for the next level without recycling similar content each year.

By second grade, chances are your students already know Martin Luther King Jr. had a dream. When we think about people who experienced the horrors of the Holocaust, we are only able to recall one name: Anne Frank. We remember learning about her in fifth grade, eighth grade, and then again in eleventh grade. Anne was so important, but we have to wonder—Who else and what else can we be teaching about? Where can we go deeper? How can we teach more?

Sociology helps kids connect to others on a human level. How can we expect our students to grow up and care about the issues that are affecting people across a border or an ocean if we never help them to connect with them *as people*? We wanted to show our students that people all over the world, not just America, are inventors and explorers. We wanted them to know that others have holidays, languages, families, cultures, and stories to tell that were worth knowing and being inspired by. Sociology lessons can help our students become more culturally aware, thus helping them to be more accepting of the differences they see in the world. When students are able to learn, discuss, and understand how and why other groups of people came to be what they are today, they can begin to build empathy and acceptance for them and gain perspective. They can see themselves reflected in others.

So how did we tackle this in the classroom for an entire year? We created lessons about a variety of cultures. We researched interesting stories, inventors, and contributions from around the world. Then we began to compile all of the information into ebooks written at a level our students could make sense of and appreciate.

Our inspiration for sociology topics sometimes comes from what we see and hear in the world. For example, we've noticed that when Black History Month or even the television network Black Entertainment (BET) is mentioned, someone will inevitably ask why specifically Black cultural institutions exist, and they'll often venture into labeling them as "racist." When we see these things happening, we typically spring into action. We see things like this as content that can be shared with students.

For example, we decided to teach our primary students about historically Black colleges and universities or HBCUs. Why? Well, in 2017 the US secretary of education, Betsy DeVos, ignorantly made the comment that HBCUs were pioneers of school choice. We saw others affirming this statement and realized that some people really don't understand how HBCUs came to be. These schools were not created to widen the pool of school choices. They were created out of necessity as a direct result of the racial segregation enforced by Jim Crow laws. Black students were not allowed to attend white colleges. There was no other choice. We have both encountered our fair share of friends and acquaintances inquiring about the purpose of HBCUs. These same people also held some misconceptions about HBCUs being racist and unnecessary.

Knowing the value of HBCUs helps students realize that these colleges and universities are here out of necessity and they are still needed today, as they are spaces where many students say they can finally see themselves reflected in the curriculum.

We didn't know that there was a yearly observation put on by the United Nations called the International Day of Persons with Disabilities. We decided to tell our students about this day and its mission, which, according to the UN website, is to "promote an understanding of disability issues and mobilize support for the dignity, rights, and well-being of persons with disabilities. It also seeks to increase awareness of gains to be derived from the integration of persons with disabilities in every aspect of political, social, economic and cultural life."

In an effort to build empathy among our students and intentionally combat Islamophobia, one of the things we did was to discuss World Hijab Day for one of our sociology lessons in February. Now, we've got to be honest: when we first attempted to educate our students about this day, we got things wrong. After talking to multiple educators about our work on social media, we were actually called out and received some pushback from a hijab-wearing Muslim educator. Our intention was to build empathy toward hijab-wearing women, but our impact was positioning them as people to be pitied. It was embarrassing and unfortunate—but it led to our growth and understanding as educators. We publicly discussed our mistake and openly apologized because we wanted people to see what it looked like to admit that you've done harm.

This experience taught us to be more cautious moving forward, but we didn't let it stop us. Along your own journey to making social studies important again, things like this are going to happen from time to time. When you are diving into new cultures and discussing the experiences of people you don't have a lot of experience with, mistakes are going to happen. This is something that just needs to be accepted. It should not be used as an excuse to avoid the work. With the world at our fingertips thanks to technology, we can expose ourselves to more, connect with people all over the world, and do better for our students. Again, we want to be clear, in the beginning, we felt a little uncomfortable and the lessons didn't always come naturally to us. We had to do a lot of research and reach out to people who had lived these experiences to make sure our own biases weren't getting in the way of teaching lessons accurately to our students. There are a few examples of lessons that were built on that kind of research that we'd like to share with you.

Celebrating Families around the Globe

"Are there any people that have Mother's Day and Father's Day like we do here?" a kindergarten student asked after a sociology lesson one day.

May is Asian and Pacific Islander Heritage Month, so we had decided to introduce our students to a special day celebrated in South Korea called Parents' Day. A few days before Parents' Day, South Koreans observe Children's Day. We learned about that too. It is a day for South Korean people to celebrate their kids. This, of course, left our students wishing they could move to South Korea so that they too could be celebrated on May 5.

With our students, we created a KWL chart in order to organize the information we were getting ready to learn about South Korea. For those that don't know, this is a chart that teachers use to keep track of what students *know*, what they *want to know*, and what they've *learned*. Some of the questions our students asked were:

- Do any other countries have Children's Day?
- Why is it Parents' Day and not Mother's Day and Father's Day?
- Why don't we have Children's Day and Parents' Day in America?

It turns out we actually do have Children's Day in the United States, and so do almost fifty other countries! What a world connection we were able to make as we explored and talked about each one. It was another great opportunity to point to our map and globe. We can still see our students racing to grab the globe and asking which continent each country could be found on. We can hear them wondering how close or far it was to where we currently were and wanting to know more about the kids who lived there. When we expose students to more, they are eager to learn more!

Global Bias and Global Excitement

One of our students' parents informed us that they were taking a trip to Nuremberg, Germany, that summer because it was all her son could talk about. During our gingerbread lesson, we had discovered that Nuremberg was known as the gingerbread capital of the world. Then, our class was lucky enough to have a fellow teacher who lived in Germany send us gingerbread and other German treats! How incredible is that? Our students couldn't believe that they were eating treats that came across the Atlantic Ocean and were from the country we had just learned about. We went back to the map and checked out all of the countries surrounding Germany. The students were jealous that kids in Poland, Austria, France, and Switzerland could just get in a car to travel to Germany and get all the gingerbread they wanted!

This prompted a brief discussion about how each of the fifty countries in Europe had their own rules about people entering into them. Authentic engagement with a map always makes our teacher hearts happy. What sticks out to us the most about that particular lesson is that we were able to introduce our students to the experiences of people from a different country in a way that made them genuinely want to know more, and it had nothing to do with showing a disparity in how things are done in America compared to a different country.

We can't remember many lessons from our own time in elementary school that left us wanting to travel to other countries. If anything, the lessons left us wishing we never ended up anywhere else and feeling sorry for anyone who had to live there. When we were growing up, the lessons and images we most often saw about other countries just made us sad that those countries weren't more like America. Looking back, it saddens us that we were not inspired to learn more about different cultures or appreciate them. We can recall seeing images of malnourished children in Africa—never a specific country, of course, which led us to believe for many years that all African countries and people were exactly alike. We were never exposed to the diverse food, languages, celebrations, landscapes, and beauty of each individual country. The lessons just lumped all Africans together, and the children were all shown in the same light: poor and in need of help from Americans—specifically white Americans. Any other time Africa was mentioned in a lesson, the discussion typically revolved around exotic animals you'd see on a safari. Africa was mentioned each and every February, but only as a place where enslaved people came from. Imagine the biases and stereotypes we and our peers built up toward the entire continent of Africa, all fifty-four countries included, because of a lack of sociology lessons that could have showed us more.

We develop biases based on what we see and experience but also based on what we do not see and experience. The only images school lessons from our childhoods showed of people from countries with predominantly Black and Brown citizens were of those who were enslaved, living in poverty, losing a war, or depicted as "savages." The lessons often showed that other countries and cultures had less to offer. We want our students to know that the world has so much more. The American way isn't the only way. The American way isn't necessarily the best way. Many other countries, cultures, and people around the world are also inspiring, thriving, and worth knowing about.

The most amazing part about teaching sociology to young students is seeing their natural curiosity about the world unfold and seeing them relate to people they would otherwise assume they had nothing in common with. When we introduce our students to people all over the globe, it helps them seek to understand others instead of simply making judgments or believing stereotypes. They begin to ask questions that matter, and you get the sense that they are being opened up to a world of more.

Different People Do Different Things in Different Ways

Día de Muertos, or the Day of the Dead, is a Mexican holiday. While it coincides closely on the calendar with Halloween, we learned that the celebrations have nothing to do with each other. Some of the families of our students shared with us that Día de Muertos is a gathering of friends and family to remember loved ones who have passed away. What our students gathered from learning about this holiday was that some Mexican people may think about death in a different way than some Americans, and that's okay. Some of our students found this hard to understand, because many of our students had only experienced death and funerals as really sad events. They noted that in America families get together after someone dies, just like in Mexico. The difference was the ways in which the dead were honored.

Most of our students loved the idea of Día de Muertos and thought it was a more meaningful way to remember their own loved ones who had passed. It was mind blowing for them when we pointed out that there are many more people who handle death and life in a number of different ways than they might be used to. In their short lives, with the small amount of experiences they'd had so far, it never occurred to them that people in other parts of the world might have really different ways of doing things. This made them curious about other ways different cultures might be different from what they knew.

A phrase we always find ourselves saying is, "Different people do different things in different ways, and that's okay." Our students eventually begin to this say to each other as the year goes on when someone asks, "Why do they do it that way?" or says "That's weird!"

Bunnies

We were also able to get some sociology into our classrooms by studying bunnies!

I'm sure you're thinking, "bunnies?" Remember, we look for the global connection in all things. In the spring, primary classrooms typically engage in thematic units around life cycles. You'll see the tiny faces of curious students hovering over caterpillars and even eggs that will hatch into baby chicks. These lessons are beloved and so much fun— but we are always looking for ways to go deeper. So, when springtime came around and we were in the middle of a unit on bunnies, chicks, and all things spring, we were searching for a connection to sociology. Research ensued, and we came across some intriguing data from a survey about chocolate rabbits, which are extremely popular during that time of year. For some (amusing) reason, someone had decided to conduct a study to figure out which part of the chocolate bunny was typically the first to be chomped off—and then proceeded to explain a theory about what that said about the chomper! This was so charming that we were immediately all over it. We knew our students would enjoy the findings of this study, and there was a social studies connection: surveys. People conduct surveys as a part of their job—as a part of life! We discussed the process: collecting samples (from a variety of subjects, of course), organizing data, and drawing conclusions. We learned that people who get curious enough are able to take action by conducting research and collecting data.

Anytime we introduce a concept such as this one, we try to give students an experience of some kind. So, as a class, we decided to get curious. Students got into groups and decided to have a conversation about ideas that they were curious about. Then they were given the chance to plan a survey to collect their data! They were able to set up tables in the cafeteria to ask fellow students to fill out a short survey about their topic. Some students wanted opinions on television shows. Other students wanted to get a pulse on how happy everyone *truly* was with the school lunch.

The latter question led to our students considering questions about the design of their survey. At first, students tried to collect data at the beginning of the lunch period, but all of the respondents that they needed were busy . . . getting their hot lunches. The only students available to collect data from were students that packed lunch from home.

As teachers, we had to talk to our students about whether or not those subjects would truly give them a pulse on the question that they were seeking to answer. The next day, they adjusted and ran their survey toward the end of lunch at a table near where the hot lunch students walked to throw their trash away. This is big work! These kinds of projects yield the higher-order thinking that everyone is begging teachers to cultivate—because they are rooted in realness. Yes, the bunnies are silly, but the concept of collecting data is not.

How can you start global sociology lessons in your classroom? Keep your eyes open for interesting topics about how people live or what people do. Did you see an interesting headline in the paper? Did you get sucked into the comments sections of a controversial article? What concept is at the root of that? Can it be turned into a classroom conversation? Can your students have an experience around that topic? Sociology is everywhere if you pay attention.

UNPACK

Incorporate sociology into all your lessons, going beyond Western cultures to include other parts of the world. Avoid repetition throughout different grade levels, and don't be afraid to take risks or go outside your comfort zone. Teach this motto: "Different people do different things in different ways, and that's okay."

IMPACT

Children have a natural curiosity about the world, and are eager to experience diverse cultures and ways of life. Sociology lessons help students connect with and build empathy for the people around and apart from them, overcoming biases and stereotypes. Students learn how to appreciate differences and bond over similarities.

CHAPTER FOUR

ECONOMICS, GEOGRAPHY, AND CIVICS IN THE PRIMARY CLASSROOM

One of the most interesting and frustrating statements we hear from teachers sounds something like this: "I love what you do. I don't teach social studies, but I love what you do." What's interesting about that is when you look up the definition of social studies, it describes literally everything that makes up how we live and how the world works. We have a little mantra that we enjoy. It goes, "If you teach humans, then you teach social studies!"

We've already covered two aspects of social studies, history and sociology. We can begin to address the others now: economics, geography, and civics. We all deal with these topics on a daily basis—so why wouldn't we teach them?

Hopefully, we are beginning to convince you of the importance of getting global at every opportunity. Our goal is always exposure. We want you to expose students to as many topics as you can because, dear teacher, you might be the only person who cracks the world open for your students! What an amazing privilege that is. People are always looking for "teachable moments"—and that's awesome—but in addition, look for globally relevant moments to teach into. Let's skip teaching a surface-level thematic unit on polar bears for the tenth year in a row and teach something authentic.

Economics

Can we really afford to wait until senior year of high school for our students to be exposed to economic concepts? Think about it: outside of the typical "wants and needs" unit or maybe the "consumer/producer" chapter in our social studies textbook (if we are lucky enough to have one), what are our students learning about economics that will serve not only them but our society in the future?

LaNesha

I remember putting off government and economics class until the last semester of senior year. I was so excited to take off and begin my new collegiate life that the government and economics class was a mere hurdle to get over. I was checked out.

My fresh-out-of-college teacher said, "We are doing a stock market project. You need to select a business or company to invest in. You'll track the stocks for two weeks and calculate your earnings and losses." I barely understood that, and quite honestly, I didn't care to understand because I was too busy daydreaming about decorating the dorm room I'd be moving into soon.

Fast forward to college. I fell for what so many students fall for: the credit card. "So, wait—I just sign this and you give me a card with a thousand dollars on it? May I have two?" I'd heard about interest, but I was never really taught about it. What did it matter? I needed money, and all I had to do was make a twenty-three-dollar monthly payment.

Fast forward again, this time to my very first teaching job. I was so thrilled to finally be a teacher. I was sent to a building to meet with some guy who joked that he'd be the one "making sure I got paid." Well, I laughed right along with him because I was thinking, "Yessss. I need that because the credit card people want their twenty-three bucks by the end of the month."

> I remember him asking me if I wanted to file zero or one. Zero or one, what? He read my hesitation and assured me "most people select zero so they can get more money back during tax season." I didn't know that meant essentially giving the government an interest-free loan. But, I did hear him say "more money," so I said, "Sign me up!"
>
> To this very day, lots of economic concepts are lost on me. While that may be my fault now, I can't help but wonder if things would be different if I'd been taught more about money early on.

Our education system takes two of the most powerful and impactful subjects—economics and government—and splits them and tosses them into a senior-year requirement. We throw these life skills at a room full of teenagers whose biggest concern is what they are about to do next in their lives. Then we wonder why one of the catchphrases of our current generation is "adulting is hard." Adulting *is* hard when you've been given little to no opportunity to learn these vital skills.

But what if our students got a continual sprinkling of relevant economic concepts starting in kindergarten? What if we began to include global economic topics in our social studies instruction? Just imagine the kind of students we would send out into the world. Think about how much more effective that senior-year stock market project would be.

Honestly, outside of teaching young children how to identify and count coins (and maybe the occasional budget-based project), when are we ever teaching children about the way money works? We read a study from an online tax company that showed that 57 percent of Americans are not confident about their knowledge of the tax code.[1] That saddens us, but we are not surprised (mostly because we are included in that 57 percent). Most of the people we know who are savvy with things

---

1   TaxSlayer, "As IRS Opens, Taxpayers Stressed over Filing but Thinking about Refunds," January 29, 2018, www.taxslayer.com/mediaroom/prdetails?articleID=122491.

like finance and investing say that they've learned a lot of it from their parents.

Now, some of you are likely thinking, "What's wrong with families teaching these skills to their children?" If that is what you are thinking, then just take a minute and consider what position one must be in in order to ask a question like that. Many studies show that wealthy parents are more likely to produce wealthy children. If you were fortunate enough to watch your parents and grandparents bring in money, spend money, and manage money, you are bound to pick up some helpful tips. Also, they will likely tell you what you should do with your money. It's a built-in perk of having generational wealth. That is not everyone's experience.

It is no wonder why there are so many Americans who are in debt and unsure about tax codes, 401(k)s, and the stock market. But what if we gave students lessons about these very critical things in the classroom? Think about what the impact could be if we exposed them to economic lessons. It could change their lives.

Practical Ideas for Getting Economics in the Classroom

We had downloaded and printed images of money from all over the world. We cut them out so that they looked like real money. We laid them all over a table for students to see when they walked in. When the students filed into class, they immediately spotted the table.

"What is this?" a student asked.

"This is money! It's currency," we responded.

Another student said, "Wait a minute! That's the queen! My mom watches her on Netflix! She has her own money?"

"She does! How cool is that?" we answered.

The student said, "I've never seen a girl on money before."

Another student said, "Wait, there's money with ANIMALS on it?"

"Yes! Isn't it beautiful?"

"Where do they get to have animals on their money? I want to go there."

We pulled out the globe and said, "It's right here. That's Tanzania. It's—"

Another student chimed in. "In Africa! I know that's Africa. Okay, so to go there we just have to get on a boat to get across the water."

"That's one way to get there!"

Every child that walked into the classroom that morning was just as fascinated as those first few students. They were intrigued about why other countries put those images on their money, and discussed it together. We arrived at the conjecture that countries must print things that are important to them on their currency. We then began to ask them about what was important to them.

One student said, "My Little Pony is the most important thing in my life. I need some My Little Pony money."

"You obviously do. What if I gave you some paper and you could get with a group and design your own currency? You can do that for morning work today, but only if you are on task."

And, boy, were they ever on task. Designing money ended up being the morning work for the rest of the week. We now had young children creating a currency system and assigning a value to the currency. They were having a kindergarten-friendly experience with a very mature concept. That's what we are after!

Economics: Money Has History!

We wanted to look at the history of money, so we decided to teach our students about bartering and trading. We set up a simulation, putting students in groups that each had a monopoly on a certain item that would be needed to complete a project. The task was to re-create a painting of a rainbow. One team had the paper, another team had some paintbrushes, another team the paint, water, and cups.

However, we were meanies: we created a surplus of some items and a deficit of others.

After we gave students their task, they excitedly took off and began to barter and trade. It was so much fun that the group with the paintbrushes didn't even realize that in all of the excitement, they'd given away all of their brushes.

"Teacher, we didn't keep a brush for our group."

"Oh, that's a problem, isn't it?"

"Yes . . . can you give us another one?"

"Oh, I'm so sorry, but that's all you have. How will you complete your task now?"

You can imagine the internal chuckling that was happening as we watched this group sit, gawking at the rest of the groups that were able to get started. They learned an important lesson about conservation that day. We repeated this activity with new groups a week or so later, and it was a very different experience! This time, the students were much more careful about their trades. Some groups were more conservative with their resources, while others planned a specific strategy to barter with other groups to meet their needs.

Economics and Thematic Units

We were also able to get some economic concepts in when teaching thematic units. Around February, we were looking for a way to shake up Valentine's Day. We got to thinking about the economics of the holiday and how flower prices get marked up right around this season. We also started wondering about where all of these flowers came from. We did some research and read about how flowers were farmed in various parts of the world. We learned that the typical working conditions for people that farm flowers are awful. That led us to reading up on fair trade policies. We thought it would be interesting to expose our students to the concept of fair trade, and the conversations around this topic were amazing. Our students wondered why the people who were producing all of the goods weren't getting paid more money when businesses could not exist without them. By the end of this lesson, we had students going home demanding that their parents find Fair Trade Certified products to purchase!

That spring, we taught our kindergarteners and first graders a unit on frogs (as most teachers do). We took frogs right through the "social studies five"—history, sociology, geography, economics, and civics. For a connection to economics, we ended up reading about a most charming tradition from Snohomish, Washington, called GroundFrog Day. GroundFrog day is celebrated in lieu of Groundhog Day. Some residents in Snohomish decided that an East Coast groundhog had no business predicting the return of spring for their West Coast weather! The residents got together and created their own tradition. It includes a frog that they have named Snohomish Slew. If Slew croaks, sunny skies for spring are near. If Slew does not, they can expect more wet weather. Frogs have a natural ability for predicting the arrival of spring: when they wake from a winter slumber, they tend to get "croaky" if spring is coming. The people in Snohomish always trust Slew's croak!

We know you are thinking, "Where is the connection to economics?" Well, the GroundFrog Day festival was also a fundraiser used to support local organizations. At one time, this festival raised money so that local Snohomish second graders could take free swim lessons! So

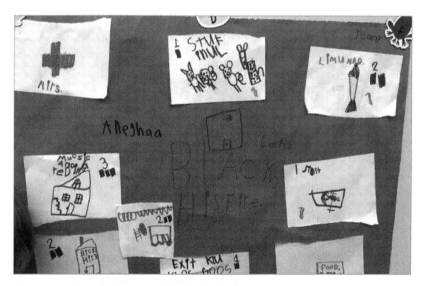

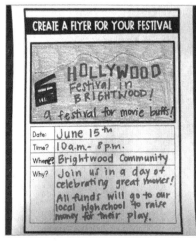

we ask students why it is important to raise funds. We discuss how special events are not just a way to raise money but also a way to promote the message and goals of a charity or an organization that depends on outside money in order to function. Events like GroundFrog Day allow people to come out and have a good time, but they also expose folks to causes that need help.

After learning about the GroundFrog Day festival, our class designed their own festivals to raise awareness and funds. We had students get in teams and decide on a theme for their festival. We provided a large piece of butcher paper that they used to plan out attractions, booths, and entertainment. They also had to pick a cause to raise funds for. Some of our students who were rarely excited to learn were now fully invested in their Superhero Festival, which would raise funds for children who didn't have any toys (oh, our hearts). Other students made a Fashion Festival that would include fashion shows and a clothing drive and would raise money for people who needed clothing. The planning, attention to detail, and execution for a project like this was an intense undertaking—but so worth it.

UNPACK

Waiting until senior year to require economics is unacceptable. Educators can work together to include these concepts from the earliest grade levels. Incorporate social studies through cultural themes to keep the lessons fun and engaging.

IMPACT

Students will grow comfortable with these concepts from an early age and be far better prepared to grasp them in detail by the time they reach senior year.

Geography: Pointing to the Globe Every Day

Quick question: Where is your classroom map? Do you have a globe? How often do you use it? Be honest. Is it in the janitor's closet because it was taking up valuable wall space?

We'll say it again: we are not judging you. We ditched our maps in our early years because we wanted to revamp our word walls and those maps just had to go. We never used them! We didn't have a social studies curriculum, so we just didn't see the point. The custodians came down, uninstalled the maps, and carted them away. Oh, how different things are now that we have decided that, as professional educators, we refuse to not teach real content. These days, we are on the map daily. We are like two Carmen Sandiegos in our classrooms. As our love for maps grew, so did our understanding of the geographical misconceptions we held. Continent locations and sizes are not accurate at all in our mental maps for a number of reasons. We were recently surprised to discover that the majority of South America is actually located to the east of Florida, Brazil is almost as big as Canada, Alaska is smaller than Libya, and Africa is bigger than Brazil, China, and the United States combined! How interesting of a lesson would all of that be for students to learn? And on top of being interesting, it's the truth—so we should teach it.

We have a friend who teaches high school, and a handful of her students had no clue where Hawaii and Alaska were located because they'd only ever seen them in boxes at the bottom of a US map. We're sure each teacher in their past assumed the grade-level teacher before or after would cover the basics. The result is students falling through the cracks.

When social studies became a part of our everyday lives at school, we constantly found ourselves looking things up on the map. As you will see later on in this chapter, we also began to look at the historical aspects of, well, everything. Math concepts, writing units, science experiments—all of these things are oozing with social studies connections. You've just got to be on the lookout!

Let's take a quick example from a math lesson that took a detour through some social studies content. One year, as we began the unit on telling time, we researched the history of timekeeping. This is one of our tricks for getting social studies in—always ask about the history of any given topic! We looked it up and discovered that there were historical records that show early timekeeping systems and devices that were developed by ancient Egyptians. We went online and found some fascinating images of Egypt and the shadow clocks developed there for a slide show so that the class could see what these brilliant people had created.

We'd previously talked about Egypt extensively when we learned about a place called 6th of October City. Previously, our students only thought about mummies, pyramids, and deserts when they thought about Egypt. After our lessons, what they wanted to know next was where Egypt was and what the culture there was like. We were on the map within minutes. After finding where we were currently located, we quickly realized that we would need to cross water to get to Egypt.

"That's the Atlantic Ocean! That's the same ocean that you said Ferdinand Magellan started his journey on!"

You probably think we're exaggerating. We can assure you that we're not. Yes, we did learn about Ferdinand Magellan back in September, and it doesn't hurt that we have a culture bulletin board in our classrooms where we post all of the amazing content we learn throughout the school year to reference whenever we need to, but more importantly, when we give students interesting, relevant, and real topics to learn about, it sticks! All of a sudden, your bright, intelligent, and capable students are making connections that you hadn't even thought of.

Our students are never more engaged then when we are delivering rich, globally and culturally relevant lessons. That's because, for once, school becomes engaging just because of content! Our students are begging for interesting content. They beg for it with their behavior and deep sighs when they have to read the same narrative about colonial times for the third year in a row. We don't find ourselves asking students to stop talking or to pay attention when they are learning this culturally relevant work. It feels like—well, it feels like teaching.

Let's get back to geography. So, yes, we made the connection to Magellan's voyage. From there, on the map, we crossed the Atlantic and ended up in Morocco. That's where we recalled our conversations around continents and countries. We skipped over to Algeria, Libya, and finally landed in Egypt—all because of a math standard. With social studies, the connections are quite literally endless.

So many teachers ask us how we have time to crack open topics like this. Well, this is a perfect example: we infused social studies into a math lesson, and it reminded our students of a Ferdinand Magellan lesson and primed them for upcoming lessons! We were able to get more in because the groundwork had been laid already. One lesson about geography served us well for the remainder of the year. We also don't have to reduce a lesson about oceans and continents to strictly that—a boring, matter-of-fact lesson labeling seas and land masses. The students learn about oceans and continents authentically as we are crossing them on the map when we are trying to figure out how to get to the area we are learning about from our current location.

So, let's dig in. How can we get geography to be a part of our everyday lessons? The first step is easy. Head down to the custodian and ask them to dig your map back out and get it posted in your classroom. Also, keep your eyes peeled for random globes laying around your school. No one's using them anyway—grab them! Then watch what happens when the world is displayed for your students. Children who have not been exposed to maps and globes are usually fascinated when they get their hands on one.

Second step: Listen. Listen in as your students are exploring. Figure out what they already know about the map. Take note of the questions that they are asking each other. Notice the vocabulary that they are using. This is a great way to ascertain their map skills and prior knowledge without doing a full-blown assessment.

Geography through Culture

Keep your eyes open for opportunities to point to the map. Remember when we explained that during the first few weeks of school, we tend to forgo the typical "all about me" activities (the bags, the posters, etc.) and instead send home a culture case? We send home a folder with labeled dividers and places for our students and families to insert information to teach us about their cultures. Well, one of the things that we always end up doing is finding places that are mentioned in our students' culture cases on the map. Inevitably, there is a child who says that their family is from another place than we are.

We've learned from these culture cases that one of our students wasn't African American like we'd assumed. That's when we ran to the globe to figure out where Jamaica was. After some quick research, our class knew where it was and what the flag looked like.

"Hey! That flag looks just like that hat you are always wearing. Is that why you wear it?" one child exclaimed. From there, they asked this student what Jamaica is like and if he had ever been there.

LaNesha

During the first few weeks of school, I had the maps and globes out for a morning exploration center. I sat in awe as one of my kindergarten students proceeded to name every single country on the map. I cannot tell you how amazing this was. This social-studies-loving teacher was fascinated and thrilled to have a student with such knowledge! But that's when a more somber fact hit me: if this were another time in my career, a pre–social studies loving time, I very well could have let an entire school year go by without ever realizing the incredible skill set this young child had because, remember, in years past, maps and globes were nowhere to be found in my classroom and really even in my school.

I remember the bright smiles I got from this student who felt so seen and proud of his knowledge. He may not have ever had the chance to teach his friends and tell us all about the flags that represented each country. He became a shining star in our classroom . . . and if it were another year or if I were another teacher, we all would have missed out on all of that. It truly makes you wonder what other things your students are coming to school with that we just don't know about because we don't allow them to come out.

Adding Humanity to Geography

Let's look back on our own social studies education. We were nineties kids. We vividly remember our social studies books—because we hated them so much! LaNesha's was a thin book that had a purple spine. It had a picture of a mountain on it and was mostly about landforms. She remembers her visceral reaction as a nine-year-old hearing her teacher say, "Get out your social studies books, class!" She smacked down her neon slap bracelet and pushed her Trapper Keeper aside to fish out that awful book. She just didn't care. She didn't care about the physical characteristics of a peninsula. Who cares about peninsulas when you live in the middle of a cornfield in Indiana? It was either that—peninsulas—or memorizing states and capitals. Naomi remembers a social studies book from her time in Seattle titled *Washington, Our Home*. The only thing she remembers about it, however, is the fact that whoever had the book before her had scribbled out the "ington" so her book just said *Wash Our Home*. That was the most interesting thing about it.

We need to break this cycle of disinterest with geography. What our teachers and textbooks didn't really include or convey was the *why*. Why did we need to know this information? Why did it matter? Now, as we set out to rethink social studies in the elementary classroom, we try to lead with the *why* for geography. Really, when you get down to it, geography affects the way we all live. It affects the buildings we build, the environmental laws that we adhere to, and the way we dress.

Based on what we learn from the culture cases, we might place student photographs near important places to them on the map to give a glimpse into a critical part of geography: humanity. We firmly believe that the moment we add humanity to geography lessons, the engagement skyrockets!

Geography through Currency

As we mentioned before, our students were fascinated with the idea that different countries put different images on their money. As soon as they figured out that there was a country in Africa that had animals on their currency, they just had to know where this country was. There we were, right back on that map. The other currency that we shared was so beautiful and different from ours that we had to identify those countries as well. A warning, though: we've been known to get a little carried away with this! We've ended up finding books, YouTube videos, and anything else that might give us more information about a country we've been staring at on a map!

Geography through Literature

Poet Lucille Clifton states that "the literature of America should reflect the children of America." We love that quote so much because she says that our literature should reflect the children of *America*—not just the children of your classroom. Building a classroom library that showcases the children of America will do wonders for your students! They will see themselves represented and have a critical chance to gain some perspective about others through literature. When we read aloud, the stories will come from various parts of the world. When this happens, of course we find these lands on the map.

We are always wondering what the weather is like, what the buildings look like, and how people navigate their daily lives in other places. Could you imagine if all of our students were exposed to these sorts of things regularly? Not just during a special unit or culture month but regularly, as in "this is just what we do at school." What kinds of students would we turn out by the twelfth grade? How would their critical thinking, empathy, and perspectives develop? That gives us chills to think about!

Cool, but how? Take a good look at your library. What books have you chosen to put in front of your students? Are they able to get some critical exposure to characters that are different from their experience? What are the texts that you use to teach comprehension? We have to consider the implications of doing two-week-long units on *Pete the Cat* or *I Know an Old Lady*. We love Pete as much as the next teacher, but Pete can't get all of our precious instructional time when we can get way more bang for our instructional buck with rich books that celebrate diversity and keep kids engaged. Get a book that can do both. Take the book *The Name Jar* by Yangsook Choi. The main character in the book is a little girl named Unhei who has just moved to America from Korea. Instead of reading a fictional book about a fictional place, we were able to learn about a real country that we could find on the map. This was great for later in the year when we learned about Parents' Day in South Korea. *Rain School* by James Rumford took us from Asia to Africa, specifically to the country of Chad, to learn about children building a school and learning lessons along the way. *Malala's Magic Pencil* can transport your kids to Pakistan, and *Lost and Found Cat* by Doug Kuntz and Amy Shrodes allows you to follow a family as they flee from Iraq to Greece. Anytime you read books that are culturally diverse, the possibilities to include geography are endless!

Anytime we read a book that mentions a city, state, country, or even a magical nonexistent place, our students are in the habit of asking, "Is that a real place? Where is it on the map? Can I go get the globe? Can we take a field trip there?" Because of this, we began to make it a point to double-check if the settings in fictional books we read are places we can point to on the map and give our students background knowledge about before reading. Being able to pull real-world connections out of a fictional text during read-alouds encourages our students to do the same when they read on their own for fun. We keep a map and a globe in the reading center in our rooms, and students are constantly trying to find a place their book just mentioned to see where it is in relation to where they currently are.

Geography through Holiday Celebrations

Thanksgiving season in elementary can be a frustrating time for teachers who are trying to be historically accurate and culturally responsive. We've talked about this season in depth in our history chapter, but what we wanted to convey here is yet another opportunity to take something like Thanksgiving and do more with it!

As we were thinking about the things that we do during this time, we got curious about supply and demand. We wondered who was raising all of the turkeys? Who was providing all of the cranberries? This was such a great opportunity to give our students an authentic experience with the US map. We can look at the map and ask questions like "Why do you think cranberries are grown here? Could it have anything to do with the water supply and the climate of the area? Not every state can have a bog." Now we have children considering the climate implications of food production! Again, we ask, what if all kids had this exposure all of the time? When it's relevant to their lives, students will be more excited to learn about it.

This kind of teaching about holidays can be simple to set up. Print out a blank map of the US. Always locate where you live first and color that state in. Then, research your favorite recipes from the holiday season and draw or glue little food icons onto the map. You might also color the water all around the US so that students can keep in mind the fact that water supply has a huge effect on the kinds of foods we grow.

The more you point to the map, the more natural map features and concepts will feel to your kids. You can even throw in mini-lessons about map keys and compasses in an organic way that is tied to a real topic. When you are teaching a lesson that requires you to jump to the map, start where you and your students are. Ask what direction you need to go to get to the place you are learning about. This would be a great time to introduce a compass so that students can learn about cardinal directions. When you show various maps, be sure to talk about what the map is showing. Ask students how everyone can be sure that certain symbols or colors mean what they think they mean as a way to introduce a discussion about map keys.

Geography through Current Events

Look at a calendar. What's about to happen that can be tied to geography?

Is daylight saving time coming up? There's geography there! You can discuss time zones and why the daylight even needs to be "saved" because of the spring and winter equinoxes. We decided to print out a blank map of the US and draw in the time zone lines. Then, as a class, we colored the time zones in different shades. We made a list of activities that we do throughout the day (wake up, eat breakfast, go to school, etc.), and then we represented them with small pictures on a strip of paper. From there, we cut slits on the sides of the time zone map so that students could pull the strip of events in a day across it. The students were able to get the concept of time zones quickly.

"Whoa! You mean when we go to lunch, kids on the West Coast are just waking up to brush their teeth? We are beating them!"

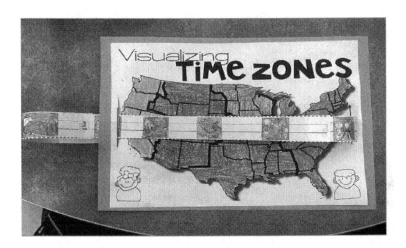

Another student wondered, "Why, though? Why can't we all be on the same time so that everything would be the same for everyone?" This called for the globe-flashlight routine. You know, the age-old experiment where you place a flashlight on a table horizontally to act as the sun while slowly turning the globe to illustrate daytime and nighttime. We discussed the need for light during the day and darkness during the night. We talked about how some jobs can only be done in the daytime, so if we were all on the same time, some people, depending on their location, would

have to go to work or even school in the dark. After discussing these implications, the need for different time zones became obvious.

What about the World Series? Who is playing who? Get out a map and find the states with teams that are in the baseball playoffs and track them as they head toward the big game. This activity is fun for family involvement because the World Series is such a big part of American culture.

Geography Can Be Practical!

Our classes spend time learning about addresses and zip codes. This can be tied into so many things. Any book about sending a letter (*A Letter to Amy* by Ezra Jack Keats, for example) would tie in. Lots of writing curriculums require you to do a friendly letter unit, so let's learn about addresses!

Did you know that zip stands for zone improvement plan? Zip codes were developed during World War II. It made sorting mail easier when a lot of the postal workers left to serve in the war. Social studies is fascinating! Hopefully, through all of these examples, you are able to see that geography is also vital. We can teach humanity, practicality, cultural exposure, and more all through the inclusion of geography.

UNPACK

Get a map for your classroom and point to it daily. Whenever you can, incorporate geography into lessons about other topics, such as reading, math, science, and current events.

> ## IMPACT
>
> Your students will become aware that there's a large world outside their immediate environment and grow accustomed to making global connections.

Civics: Priming Students for Informed Civil Discourse

Earlier in this chapter, we talked about the fact that we wait too long to teach economics concepts. Here, again, we are asking a very similar question: Can we afford to wait until senior year to teach children important concepts—concepts that matter—about the government? Think about it: so many schools wait until the twelfth grade to take two of the topics most applicable to life (government and econ) and *split* them into a single senior course. They don't even get the full year of focus they deserve! So, again, we have a classroom full of seniors who are more than likely already checked out and mentally moving on to college, a trade program, the military, or working life—sounds like a perfect time to teach about checks and balances, right?

Let's take a quick quiz. No phoning your friend Google for help. Your goal is 10/10. Ready?

1. Name all of the branches of government.
2. Who is in charge of the executive branch?
3. What do we call the first ten amendments to the US Constitution?
4. How many years is a US Senator elected for?
5. Who makes federal laws?
6. Who does a US Senator represent?
7. How many amendments has the US Constitution had?
8. Who is the chief justice of the United States Supreme Court at this very moment?

9. How many voting members does the House of Representatives have?
10. When was the Constitution written? (Hint: It's not 1776.)[2]

How'd you do? We've given this basic quiz to our friends and family, and the only ones who came even close to answering all the questions correctly were friends who are "into" politics! Everyone else was just embarrassed. But should they be? Considering the lack of attention to civics education offered in most schools, it doesn't seem surprising.

Every year, a Constitution Day survey is conducted for the Annenberg Public Policy Center of the University of Pennsylvania by an independent research company, and we can tell you, the results are a hoot. We've followed this survey for a few years now. Some fun finds: typically, only about a third of the Americans surveyed are able to name all three branches of our government, and more than a fifth can't name any. One year, more than a third couldn't name even one right guaranteed by the First Amendment, and more than half responded that it was correct to say that undocumented immigrants do not have any rights under the US Constitution (they do).

It's sort of fun to chuckle at these results until you realize that they're actually quite terrifying and disheartening. If we are to be a democracy, we need to have informed citizens! This is serious business. So serious that in 2019 Congress considered dedicating thirty million dollars

"to innovative civics learning and teaching" for all grade levels, according to the Annenberg Public Policy Center. We can do better than a senior year civics sampling for an extremely important part of our lives as Americans.

We believe that we can and should start now. In kindergarten. Imagine it! Imagine kindergarteners who may not yet understand the complex intricacies of the government but *do* understand that it is a thing. Kindergarteners are capable of understanding that there is a group of people who form something called Congress where we get laws passed. They understand that there are these three things that divide up the US government, and each has a special job to help the country run. Imagine primary students discussing the Bill of Rights or duties of the president. What would happen if every year we advanced students who were ready to learn a new layer of the inner workings of the government? Would they become more involved in their local communities? Would we see a surge in voter participation? We think so. We think that teachers can cultivate a generation of students who are willing and able to hold their leaders accountable!

We have some ideas about what it would look like to implement civics education from the primary grades. It would mean thinking about a few things: It would have to first take into account what our state standards are asking us to teach. Then we'd need to look at what students will be asked to do when they are in the upper grades and what is currently going on in the country.

Imagine sending our kids off to middle school without any phonics, reading, or basic math skills. They'd flounder! A strong foundation is key for setting our students up to be successful citizens. We can't tell you how many middle school teachers have reached out to us to thank us for giving primary students a basic understanding of some of the more complex topics they have to cover later on. Some have been outright shocked at the lack of knowledge some of their students arrive to sixth grade with. Instead of diving into a lesson that compares and contrasts the rights of American citizens to the rights of people under the rule of a dictator, they have to back up and first teach them what it even means to be a citizen. They have to pull out their maps and show them where America is even physically located. We must always ask ourselves: what if they don't get this content in the next grade level? Why can't it be us—now?

| Civics Ideas |

During that same frog unit where we learned about festivals and fundraisers, we also learned about environmental law because of the laws in place to protect exotic frogs from being taken from the rain forest and sold illegally. In our class, our students learned that because different places have different natural makeups, environmental laws vary from place to place. But who gets to decide these laws? Who decides things like laws, holidays, and observations? Enter Congress. We watched videos, looked at photos, and identified the building where Congress meets.

We decided to turn our classroom into Congress and vote on some environmental laws of our own. We placed a hopper (the wooden box that's attached to the clerk's desk in the chamber) on the teacher's desk, and students worked in teams to create new environmental laws. We

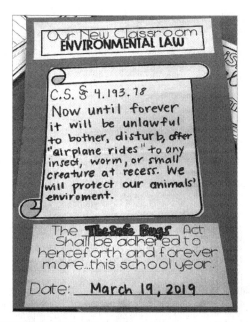

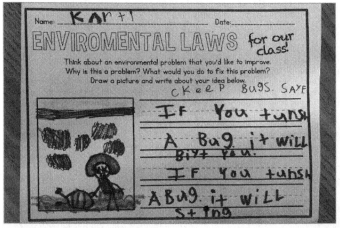

proposed bills regarding the obscene amount of soap and paper towels that we were using and how that hurt our environment. We ended up passing the Safe Bug Act of 2018. This law protects the bugs at recess from going on kindergarten "airplane rides"—the students had been actually picking up the bugs that they found on the playground and running around with them pretending they were giving them an airplane ride—that often resulted in their deaths. We decided to pass a law that required all students to leave living things alone at recess.

The Bill of Rights in Primary

"You mean, you cover the Bill of Rights in kindergarten?" We hear this often. But we sure do! Why not? Kindergarten students can know that the Bill of Rights exists. We go through the amendments one by one. Yes, even the right to bear arms. Why? Because we've lost the privilege of pretending that gun violence isn't something to talk about. That bubble was popped in Indiana in 2018 when there was a shooting in a neighboring school district. The news coverage was everywhere. Students were scared. It had to be talked about. When the right to bear arms came up, we had students debating whether or not weapons belonged in schools.

"I think we should have guns because if bad guys come, we can protect ourselves!" one student exclaimed. "No, I think that there should be no guns at all because then no one can hurt each other!" These children were going back and forth with civil discourse, and they were doing better than any adults in the comments section of a social media outlet. During these class debates, the teacher's job is only to facilitate. We don't add our own opinions or try to sway anyone, even when it is tempting. We are there to help kids stay on topic and respectful, to keep the debate going, and to make sure everyone's voice is heard. We want students to realize it's okay to change your mind if new facts or ideas compel you to do so.

| Civics and Thematic Units |

During our gingerbread unit, we decided to cover some civics. In our research, we had come across the largest gingerbread house ever created. It is twenty-one feet high, almost the size of a tennis court, located in Bryan, Texas, and made up of 35.8 million calories! It is so big, they actually had to have a building permit to begin construction! That was the spark that led us to learn more about local governments. We drive by our local government buildings all the time, so why not learn about them? We spent time learning about the role that local government plays in our lives—specifically, with building permits. So, like every year, we were going to build our gingerbread houses, but students were not issued any building materials until they applied for and secured a permit that was issued by the local government at our schools—which was us! We fully reserved the right to approve or deny any plans for construction due to safety or health concerns. Once the permit was secured, it had to be posted during construction to avoid penalties.

We've had teachers replicate this activity, but they actually sent their building permit applications to the local government. A school in Gardendale, Alabama, was surprised to see their mayor, Stan Hogeland, come and hand deliver building permits for gingerbread construction! Other teachers have been interviewed and had their classes covered on their local news stations when they've filed their gingerbread permits! What an impression that must have made on those students. They'll probably never forget that day. Real topics yield real experiences. It's amazing.

When many classes are making snowmen during a winter unit, we are too. Our snowmen are built in order to display our new winter law! This activity was a follow-up to learning about some surprising winter laws that we had learned about. For example, we found that throwing a snowball is illegal in Provo, Utah. In Michigan, a man was issued a ticket for warming his car up unattended. In Philadelphia, the police department had to create a "No Savesies" campaign to stop people from saving parking spaces with household items after they'd shoveled snow out of them! These laws were so much fun to read about, we were inspired to come up with our own winter laws. Some laws included the Hot Chocolate Act, which states that hot chocolate must be served upon returning inside from the snow. There was also the Miniature Snowman Act, which states you may not do anything outside without building a tiny snowman first.

Giving students access to civics is critical. If we can get students to be aware, learn about, and eventually act upon civic concepts that govern the way we live, we will be better as a society for it. We can set the stage for informing citizens—beginning in kindergarten.

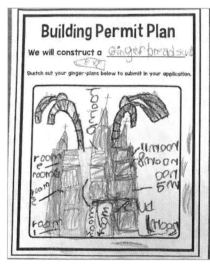 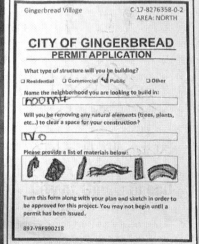

UNPACK

Teach students earlier about the basic concept of laws and government. This content is too important to wait until senior year to tackle. Engage kids with creative civics lessons such as classroom debates, voting on bills, and applying for building permits.

IMPACT

You will prepare students to understand more complex civics concepts later and hopefully inspire them to become more educated, engaged citizens.

CHAPTER FIVE

RETHINKING THEMATIC UNITS

W‌e are going to talk about thematic units: the apple unit, the gingerbread unit, the units that we know and love and that have been taught for decades. Before we dig into this chapter, just take a deep, cleansing breath, and tell yourself: *They are not trying to take my thematic units away.* Whew. Feel better? In all seriousness, we completely understand how important thematic teaching is. The connections ... the FUN! We get it. We are not trying to take your thematic units away, we just have some ideas that we hope will serve as a springboard for more as you work with your team of teachers.

Here is the cadence for how we approach a thematic unit. We start by asking ourselves a few questions:

- How will this unit help a student grow as a global learner?
"If we are learning about gingerbread, how will this show up in real life?"

- What did our students learn about this topic last year?

"Do most students probably already know how a seed grows?"

- What are they likely to learn about it next year?

"What will students learn about trees in the second grade?"

- Why is this theme so important? How could it be more important?

"It's springtime! Time to teach frogs. What is it about the frog that is so critical that we teach it year after year?"

- Where are some connections to real-life events, people, or issues?

"It's Valentine's Day. We could do the same crafts about flowers, or we could learn about how they're bought and sold!"

It took time to change our way of thinking, but now we can't help but think about thematic units in this way, and questions like these inform the way we look at everything. We look at the privilege of educating students for 180 days as a serious mission. Every lesson is an opportunity to plant a seed that might grow into a new way of thinking or understanding. Every topic is a chance to show students a world beyond the one they see daily.

We would like to walk through a few units with you so that you can get into our heads and thought processes. We hope we can inspire you to look at your own thematic units through a different lens. We use the five subtopics of social studies—history, sociology, economics, geography, and civics—to think through thematic units. We also try to think about science/STEM topics that can be global.

Apples and STEM

It started as a joke.

In 2018, we were presenting at a conference in Nashville for educators who create resources for students. In between sessions, we were looking for clip art of apples and pumpkins to add to our presentation. At this point, we were just trying to encourage teachers to consider moving past teaching the same topics year after year. As we searched, Naomi came across a website with a nice apple image. On the web page, there was a list of random facts about apples. She casually skimmed the list and said, "Did you know that apple seeds originated in Asia?" We jokingly started to talk about how we should create an apple unit. For years at that point, we had poked fun at traditional apple units. But the more we talked, the more we realized we were on to something! We already had figured out a geography connection, so we began to see if we could find connections to the other social studies topics . . . and boy, did we ever.

We decided to write the apple unit, but it was not just any apple unit: we created our first Not Your Average Unit. Our Not Your Average Units take a traditional theme or topic and reimagine it through social studies. We research the theme and one of the social studies topics like history, sociology, or economics, and see what we can find.

We also like to search for the theme and words like "controversy" or "little known facts" to get some cool connections. This was one of our most interesting finds in regard to apples. After searching "apples and controversy," an article came up that caught our eyes. The headline read, "Are Your Apples Really Fresh?" We absolutely needed to figure out what that was about.

The controversy was real. The article was all about how some people were really upset after learning that the apples they were purchasing in supermarkets could potentially be up to a year old. Crazy, right? Upon further research, we learned that the industry harvests the apples and then keeps them in temperature-controlled rooms for months at a time! Sometimes people in the industry even call these "birthday apples" because they're so old!

Some people even tested the apples to see if there were any nutritional losses. They found that there were. Studies showed that the longer an apple sits, the lower its antioxidant levels are. Consumers felt as though the supermarkets should not advertise fruit that is a year old and not as nutritionally sound as "fresh fruit." Naturally, we found this fascinating. There were so many connections to be made!

We discussed the pros and cons of freezing apples. We debated—a lot! Some of our students were on team "Apples all year no matter what," while others were on team "Fresh apples only, please." It was really fun to hear five- and six-year-olds defend their reasoning for fresh vs. frozen apples. We decided to turn it into a science experiment. We spent some time freezing apples and discussing why our freezers changed the apples so much but the professional apple-storage rooms didn't. We even kept an apple in the refrigerator for weeks and weeks to see if it kept better than an apple that was kept at room temperature.

We love to turn information about things happening in the world into classroom content. With some pictures and PowerPoint, you can create a slide show in minutes! This can serve as a way for your students to gain access to information and process it through questions and lots of turn-and-talk sessions (when students sit with partners and have a conversation).

Apples and History

When it came time to teach a historical topic related to apples, we found ourselves running around and around Johnny Appleseed. It was the obvious choice, but we were going for originality. After coming up with a lot of dead ends, we decided to give old Johnny a try. Typically, when teachers teach about Johnny Appleseed, they follow a similar narrative. Students learn about folktales and storytelling. The teacher shares the tale of a kindhearted man in tattered clothing who walked all over Pennsylvania, Ontario, Ohio, Indiana, and Illinois. He wore a pot on his head and a satchel full of seeds so he could plant apple trees all over and people would have apples to eat. Some people even say he could talk to the animals and that he was a friend to the "Indians."

This story has charmed classrooms for decades, as is evident in the numerous books and videos dedicated to his legacy. We believe that legends and folktales were meant to be shared. However, we did find some extremely interesting information that could give students some new ideas to consider.

Johnny Appleseed was a real person. His name was John Chapman. However, we shouldn't let the stories of tattered clothing fool us into thinking that he was poor. We learned that there are many accounts that would actually label John Chapman as quite the savvy businessman. He actually died a very wealthy man. Old Johnny was privy to a certain piece of information: a law that stated that if you planted an orchard and developed a piece of land, you could claim that land as your own! The reason Johnny went around planting as many trees as he could might have been that he had also figured out that all of the settlers who were arriving needed land to live on. And another fun fact: apparently, he didn't trust banks. He buried his money underground! We were also taught that he carried a satchel of seeds to plant trees everywhere for people to eat, but there's more to that as well. The fact is that the apples from those trees weren't best suited for eating. People learned to harvest the apples for lots of reasons, but, as it turns out, snacking wasn't really the main one. They were actually very useful for making alcoholic beverages!

We can assure you, when the content is interesting, you don't have to fight for student engagement. Students' mouths are typically hanging open in wonder when we read stories like this.

Apples and Sociology

As we were researching all things apples, we learned something that, in retrospect, should have been obvious: every single apple that we purchase is picked by hand. If you didn't already know that, it's sort of daunting to think about how the thousands of apples we see are passed through human hands. But then you think, "Well, I've never seen an apple picking machine." We started reading about apple farms and the job description of an apple picker.

We were shocked to learn that these workers are typically required to fill anywhere from seven to nine bins that can hold up to nine hundred pounds of apples *every day*! Many apple pickers are migrant workers. That was a huge point we wanted to cover: what is a migrant worker? We talked about what it meant to move to another place to get a job and why people have to do that. Another interesting thing that we read about was how some farmers were having a hard time harvesting the apples because so many migrant workers in recent years have been fearful to come to the United States due to immigration restrictions. While we did not get into the civics of that particular piece of information, the connections to civics are vast!

Apples and Economics

Honestly, when researching the combination of apples and economics, we weren't hopeful. Of course, we were inundated with articles about the economics of Apple *products*: iPhones, iPads, and every other manner of "iThings" out there. Then, as we kept reading, we came across an article entitled "America's Favorite Fruit." We nearly skipped it because we thought, "Well, duh—that's the apple. What's more American than apples?" But something told us check it out. Suddenly we were knee-deep in data, charts, and spending trends. Turns out the apple is *not* America's favorite fruit . . . it's actually the banana! As we read about seasonal, regional, and all other kinds of spending trends, we had a huge question: whose job is it to know this stuff? And just like that, our economics connection was there. It was market research!

We could teach our students about the fact that there are people who track spending habits, not just for fruit but for everything. We could teach them that this research is critical for our economy, that it can inform business owners, vendors, farmers, and the list goes on. We created a slide show with images that our primary students could access to get an understanding of market research.

Now, with anything like this, we are obviously not going for mastery of content. This is about exposure. We are just planting seeds of real-life concepts that will inevitably come up again because they are things that we deal with in the real world. Honestly, that's the best part of this work. Because the topics are so relevant, it is not uncommon for our students to say things like, "Hey, we learned about the Silk Road when you taught us about apples!"

But once our students have a general understanding of a topic—market research, in this case—we always try to give them some sort of experience with the concept. We decided to ask our students to predict spending trends for five different kinds of fruit. We gave them little pictures of fruit and asked them to rank them from most popular to least popular. At this point, we turned into Tyra Banks from *America's Next*

Top Model. We were all: "In my hands, there are five photographs. These photographs represent the fruits that are still in the running for becoming America's top fruit."

We dramatically revealed the fruits one at a time, and the students (who had mostly selected the apple as the most popular fruit) were shocked to learn that it's actually the banana! Now, let us remind you: we teach kindergarten, and we've taught apple units for years. We can say with absolute certainty that none of those lessons gave us the level of engagement and interest from students as the economic lesson on market research.

Apples and Geography

At the beginning of this chapter, we mentioned that apples started in Asia, and we want to show you what we did with this information. Remember, we are always looking for ways to point to the map. We researched how apples spread out to the rest of the world, and we read all about the Silk Road. We shared this information with a friend who had majored in history, and she couldn't believe we'd never really heard about this before. She lectured us on how the Silk Road was the start of global commerce and how critical it was for so many important historical events.

We couldn't wait to trace this on a map and show our students how people bartered and traded on this route from 130 BCE until 1453 CE. We learned that it was called the Silk Road more recently in history because silk made up a large proportion of trade on the route. We talked about how the apple seeds could have been traded or even dropped along the way but somehow the tree eventually made its way to other parts of the world. We talked about how people back then didn't have cars or trucks, which led to talking about how long it would take to travel the Silk Road. There were so many conversations to be had! So many connections were made—and those connections will only grow as the learning continues.

That was fun, right? Let's do it again. This time the category is pumpkins!

Pumpkins and STEM

There's something about autumn that makes us crave all things pumpkin. We have pumpkin-spice lattes with their very own release date (and a hashtag), pumpkin-spice bread . . . they even sold a pumpkin-spice toothpaste at one point! We started to wonder about the sociology behind this. Could there be a scientific explanation about why we are all purchasing pumpkin-spice lip gloss on Amazon? We found some interesting offerings that were worth exploring not only on our own but also with our students!

Some scientists say it all comes down to smell. Dr. John McGann is a sensory neuroscientist at Rutgers University who talks about how our olfactory system (our sense of smell) forms a large part of our habits and decisions (like drinking five to seven pumpkin-spice lattes a week). In oversimplified terms, when we smell pumpkin spice, it triggers memories of the fall in our brains—the crisp air, the beautiful colors, frolicking in the leaves . . . This can cause an emotional response that is pleasant for many people. Retailers have caught on to the power of olfactory memories and have certainly capitalized on it, thus the pumpkin-spice dog food.

So how did we get this information to our primary students? We decided to teach them about their sense of smell in a fresh way. We taught them about olfactory memories by conducting a science experiment. We gathered some items that might invoke a memory from their smell, things like candles and lotions. We set up a smelling lab and gave the children science notebooks to draw or write what they thought about when they smelled each item. A vanilla candle brought memories of birthday cake and therefore a favorite birthday party. Sunscreen reminded students of the swimming pool. A pumpkin-spice candle made students draw pictures of pie at a Thanksgiving table. It was a quick, easy, and inexpensive way to give students a lesson around pumpkins with a scientific twist!

Pumpkins and History

We thought about the history of pumpkins and quickly arrived at the jack-o'-lantern. We carve and decorate pumpkins year after year, but where did that tradition come from? The origins are, of course, in folklore. We begin by teaching our students that *folklore* refers to the traditional beliefs and stories of a community passed through the generations by word of mouth. Once students understand this, then they can understand that there is no real way to prove the accuracy of these stories.

The history of the jack-o'-lantern is far too dark and spiritual for the primary classroom, but it's an interesting tale for now! The Irish are responsible for bringing the tradition of carving pumpkins into jack-o'-lanterns to America, but they didn't always use pumpkins. It was common to see rutabagas, gourds, turnips, potatoes, or beets hollowed out with a candle inside. As the story goes, the original jack-o'-lantern was not a pumpkin but a person.

There are tons of versions of this story, but one popular account begins with a man named Stingy Jack. Apparently, Stingy Jack was a hateful drunkard who created chaos everywhere he went. One day, he tricked the Devil into climbing up a tree. Then he quickly placed crosses all around the tree, which meant the Devil could not come down. He made a deal with the Devil: if Jack let the Devil come down, the Devil had to promise not to take Jack's soul when he died. The Devil agreed and got to come down.

Years later, Stingy Jack died. Obviously, he was rejected from entering heaven—but he also couldn't enter hell due to the arrangement he'd made with the Devil. He was stuck between worlds, left to wander for the rest of eternity. Since there was no light in hell, the Devil tossed him a piece of burning coal inside of a hollowed turnip. From that point on, Stingy Jack was known as Jack of the turnip and eventually . . . Jack o'Lantern! In order to ward off Jack, people began to place carved-out turnips and gourds with lights set inside of them in their windows. When the Irish began to emigrate in the 1800s, they carried this tradition with them. Eventually, they realized that it was much easier to carve out a pumpkin!

Since we didn't want to be fired or be a featured controversy on the six o'clock news, we decided to not teach this whole piece of folklore in kindergarten. We told the story carefully, focusing on how people had used turnips as jack-o'-lanterns. We did tell students about Stingy Jack, but it didn't get much further than him being "not very nice to people" as we were *not* about to get into a conversation about heaven, hell, and the Devil. We know that students can handle the truth about some topics, but when it comes to a story like this, some things would be inappropriate to teach at this age.

Pumpkins and Sociology

What in the world would connect pumpkins to sociology? We came across a very interesting practice that lots of people take part in: extreme gardening. These are the people who attempt to grow the largest fruits or vegetables—including pumpkins—possible. There is often a contest of sorts where the pumpkins are evaluated on a set of criteria. These pumpkins have been turned into pies big enough for a whole town. Sometimes, they're even hollowed out enough to be turned into boats for racing!

We quickly realized that for many people, this was a way of life and a very big deal. For these people, growing a pumpkin this large can be a hobby or even a job. They might do it to be competitive or just to make people smile.

Courtesy of Samantha Kearns

We love looking at why people do what they do. That's humanity. Things that happen in the real world that communities can take part in, to us, are often worthy of being shared with students. We are always looking for opportunities to peek into the lives of others. A big reason for this is empathy. We believe that the more exposure we give our students to the world at large, the more opportunities they will have to gain perspectives they might not have otherwise considered. This is one way students are able to gain empathy. A pumpkin festival can lead to considering the notion that something one person might deem silly or unnecessary is a way of life for another.

We took this information to the classroom by sharing the idea that some people partake in XTREME GARDENING! (Every time you say it with your students, sound like you're the host of a super intense extreme-sports show!) We studied the strategies, methods, and even the history of growing extreme pumpkins. We learned about how the seeds and soil have to be tended to, and how the growers have to cover the pumpkins with a tarp for so many hours a day to protect them from the elements. There was much to discover, and it was really interesting to research—but how would we go about giving students an experience with this?

We decided to see who could "grow" the biggest pumpkin in the class . . . using paper! Each team was given a sheet of paper, scissors, and an adhesive (glue or tape). The objective was to create the largest pumpkin possible with only the materials that were given to them. This became very competitive very fast. The students began to think outside of the box after a few of them realized that you can get a pumpkin much bigger than the paper by rounding out the edges, dividing the cutout shape into halves, and extending those onto each side.

Pumpkins and Economics

We decided to look at the economics of pumpkins by learning about commodities. Commodities are the raw materials humans use to create a world that we can live in as consumers. Most agricultural commodities are the building blocks for the food that we eat. Items that are agricultural commodities are generally standardized or streamlined (people know what to expect), predictable (producers are able to produce a certain amount without too much worry), and transportable. No value is added to a commodity (a pumpkin is a pumpkin regardless of the farmer), and all commodities of the same good sell at roughly the same price.

So how could we give our students a hands-on experience with this concept? We decided to create a simulation. This experience focused on the part about goods being streamlined and standardized. Pumpkins are one commodity where having a standard version and predictable supply are important. This is because most pumpkins are purchased for decoration, as jack-o'-lanterns. Most people have a mental prototype of the "perfect pumpkin" floating around in their heads as they go shopping for one. Farmers who want to capitalize on that market are wise to make sure they grow that particular pumpkin! We wanted our students to understand that long ago, farmers became clear on the fact that one particular kind of pumpkin was popular during the fall, specifically, the Connecticut field pumpkin.

We decided to create a slide show explaining the basics of commodities. Then we told our students, "You are now members of a special pumpkin-production team. The teacher will be the supervisor and get special phone calls from your manager, who will tell your team what the pumpkins will need to be marketable." The project went a little like this:

The Pumpkin Production Experience

We wanted to give students a chance to have an experience with the idea of goods becoming a commodity. Items that are agricultural commodities are generally standardized or streamlined (people know what to expect), predictable (producers are able to produce a certain amount without too much worry), and transportable. No value is added to a commodity (a pumpkin is a pumpkin regardless of the farmer) and all commodities of the same good sell at roughly the same price. This experience focuses on the part about goods being streamlined/standard! We want students to understand that long ago, farmers became clear on the fact that a particular pumpkin was popular during this time of year. The Connecticut Field Pumpkin is the most popular pumpkin. Consumers buy them to decorate and turn into jack-o-lanterns. Most people have a mental prototype of the "perfect pumpkin" floating around in their heads as they go shopping for a pumpkin. Farmers that want to capitalize on that market would be wise to make sure they grow that particular pumpkin!

After reading the ebook, you will tell your students that they are now a member of a special pumpkin production team. You will be the supervisor and get "special phone calls" from your manager who will tell your team what the pumpkins will need to be marketable.

At the end of this experience, we hope that your students will visually see how something can be varied and then intentionally streamlined to have a great impact on production.

The Pumpkin Production Experience

To prep this activity:

1. Fold 11x17 sheets of orange construction paper (or any color in half).
2. Glue the cover (shown below) on the front.
3. Staple the pumpkin pages 1,2, and 3 on the inside.

The Pumpkin Production Experience

Say to your class:

"You are a pumpkin production team. I'm your supervisor. Your task is to draw pumpkins that we can grow so that people will buy them. You have three opportunities to draw a mock-up of the pumpkin.

"Even though we are one team, we will be more successful if we work individually! You will work under the top flap of your production design book! Are you ready? We only have three tries, so let's start on the last page and save the first page for our 1st place version!

"Turn to the last page, it will say '3' on it. Here are your directions:

1. Draw some pumpkins! Draw cool pumpkins that people will definitely want to buy! You can make them however you'd like! Make about 5 pumpkins that you think consumers will love." After everyone has drawn 5 pumpkins, have them hold them up and look at everyone's design! Hopefully they are colorful and varied in size. Make a big deal about how nice and different they all look.

*Be dramatic. Pretend you've received a call from your "manager" (I use my cellphone). As you talk aloud, say something like, "What?! What do you mean? So your latest market research shows that consumers want pumpkins that are bright orange with a good size brown stem. Oh dear. We will try again! "

Here are four samples from the first round. The pumpkins are all different.

The Pumpkin Production Experience

Say to your class:
2. "Class! We have to try again. Please turn to page two and draw your five pumpkins again. This time, we need them to be bright orange with a brown stem. The market research shows that consumers that will buy the pumpkins like for them to look a certain way. The consumers don't want them decorated after all! They would prefer them to be plain so they fit their decorations."

Allow your students some time to draw the next set of pumpkins. As they are working, remind them that they need to make sure they are now orange with a brown stem.

*Make that imaginary phone call again! Be as dramatic as you can! Say something like, "WHAT?! You mean to tell me that the consumers still aren't happy with the pumpkins we've produced? They also want them to be around the same size?! Oh, they want them to be big and round so that they can carve a really great jack-o-lantern in them? Alright then. We will give it one more shot!"

Here are four samples from the second round. They are now all orange but varied in size

The Pumpkin Production Experience

Say to your class :
"Class! We have to try again. Please turn to page 1 –the first page and draw your five pumpkins ONE more time. This time, make sure they are still bright orange with a brown stem, AND don't forget that they need to be big, round, and about the same size."

After students have drawn their third and final version, call the team over for a meeting. I have my students sit in a circle. Say, "On the count of three, show your final version (version #1) to the whole class." Ask them what they notice. (Hopefully they notice that most of their pictures look similar...especially compared to everyone's first version. Say: "Team, what we have done is listened to our consumers. We got feedback from market research and we made sure our product would make the consumer happy. In order to be a commodity, we have to make sure our product is predictable, standard (that means similar in design), and easy to replicate! We've all made a similar design for our pumpkins and I'll bet if you came to school tomorrow and I asked you to draw these again, you could easily do so. That is one way a product or a good can become a commodity!

Possible Discussion Questions:
1. Let's look at the first pumpkins that we all made on page #3. Why would the pumpkins on page #3 not work if we wanted to sell as many as we could to our consumers?
Because in order for pumpkins to be a commodity, they would need to be fairly standard (or similar) so that consumers would know what they would be able to buy.
2. Do you think it is important to listen to consumers?
If you want to be profitable/successful, then yes!

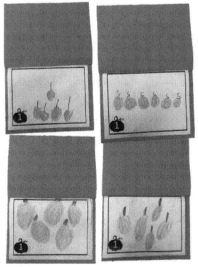

This is the final version. Most of them are similar. The students were surprised to see that all of their pictures looked very close to each other.

At the end of this experience, we wanted our students to see how something can start varied and then be intentionally streamlined to have a great impact on production and sales.

Pumpkins and Geography

Teaching geography while studying pumpkins was easy once we realized an interesting thing: you can't grow a pumpkin in Antarctica! We posed this statement as a quandary for our students. As a class, we started to talk through what we already knew about the different continents (these are the things you can talk about when your students have been exposed to geography!). Then, we did a little research (meaning we pulled up some articles from a kid-friendly search engine) to see if we could figure out why pumpkins grow on all of the other continents but not Antarctica. Naturally, we also had to list the conditions necessary for growing pumpkins. We realized that pumpkins need certain types of weather conditions to grow, and the students were able to prove this idea with the facts they'd learned from their research. This is also how

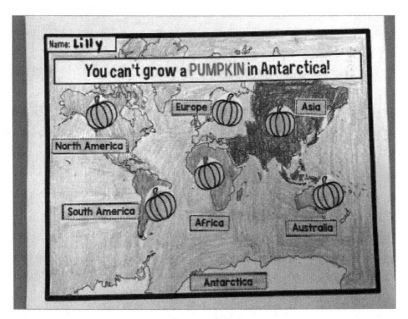

you end up with parent emails telling you how the conversation about "harsh growing environments for growing pumpkins in the wrong climate" became the topic of conversation at the dinner table that night.

Again, here come the connections! We've been talking about the economics of pumpkins, and students now understand the idea of commodities. What does that mean for Antarctica? Then more questions come! Do people in Antarctica get to carve jack-o'-lanterns? How do they get there? If they get sent there, how do they know how many pumpkins to send? As you can imagine, we *love* thinking like this. We love questions that build on other questions. We want to cultivate curiosity. This is what we are always after.

We've walked through two thematic units in this chapter with the hope that you will implement similar ideas with other thematic units across your year. Keep your eyes open! What's going on in the world? Even small things (like pumpkin-spice lattes) can evolve into a lesson and be a powerful springboard into bigger thinking!

UNPACK

In addition to "fun and cute," what greater impact can your thematic units have on your students? Try to incorporate an aspect of social studies in unit lessons whenever possible.

IMPACT

Students will see beyond the unit or theme they're discussing and understand how history, sociology, economics, and other subtopics connect to other themes.

CHAPTER SIX

SOCIAL STUDIES
AND STEM

STEM: Science, technology, engineering, and mathematics. STEM didn't tiptoe its way into American elementary classrooms. It roared. It blazed! We remember the STEM explosion well. Suddenly, in 2012, STEM was everywhere—educational-conference sessions, blogs, Pinterest, social media. Teachers and students were constructing catapults that launched aluminum foil balls across the room; teams of students were building newspaper towers that could hold extreme amounts of weight; classes constructed rafts from straws that were strong enough to float Lego people down a pond in a sensory table. It all looked like so much fun! Plenty of schools were doing STEM (or versions of it) several years before this, but as we all know, once an idea hits social media, it spreads like wildfire, and that happened with STEM.

We wanted a piece of the STEM action too. We pulled out red plastic cups, rubber bands, and anything else we could think of that would allow our students to construct something in the name of engineering. But we quickly realized that all of our STEM efforts were spiraling. Our STEM journey at this point could best be summed up in three emojis:

First we were in love and got caught up in all the fun. Then we were a little confused. Are we doing this right? Is there more to this? Then we were just plain over it. We just didn't see the point. Here's what you need to know about our teaching style: we teach with urgency. We hate wasting even one of the days that we have with our students. As renowned leadership expert and principal Baruti K. Kafele says, "I like to think I am a teacher on a mission, not just a teacher on the job."

Why is this important? It's important because after setting up a myriad of STEM experiences in our rooms, we took a step back (ducking out of the way of a few airborne aluminum foil cannonballs) and realized that we'd become so smitten with the idea of STEM that we'd failed to connect any real purpose to the challenges. We weren't doing STEM lessons that were preparing our students for real life. They were just fun for the sake of fun. We knew we had to figure it out but didn't quite know how to do it.

LaNesha

My principal called the faculty together on a teacher work day to do some planning for the second half of the year. She sat us down in teams and told us we needed to make science more of a priority, so we were to map out the rest of the year with weekly STEM challenges. A wave of heat rolled over me because I knew I would struggle with this after coming off of the prior STEM failure in my room. There was no way I could do STEM lessons if I couldn't teach my students something during the process.

She gave us a planning sheet for January through August and asked us to sketch out the remainder of the year for science. My team of kindergarten teachers went to work immediately, pulling out laptops and cell phones. They headed straight for—you guessed it—Pinterest. "Oh my gosh, how cute is this? We can do a leprechaun-trap STEM challenge for March! That'll be so much fun!" That pretty much sums up how we spent the next thirty minutes. Sure, it would be fun, but I had already experienced the aftermath of a STEM challenge without a meaningful connection. So I just sat there.

My team members asked me what was wrong. I explained that there was nothing "wrong," but I needed to figure out how to make STEM work in my classroom. One team member told me to just think about what I'd be teaching in January for social studies. That was the key!

We pumped the brakes on the STEM challenges until we returned from winter break. Then we started to fill in our January topics:

- Week One: Economics—Seasonal jobs
- Week Two: History—How did January get its name?
- Week Three: Sociology—Who was Alfred Nobel and what is the Nobel Peace Prize?
- Week Four: Civics—Who gets to decide our holidays?

We jotted those topics down on the planner and started thinking. We looked up our unit on Alfred Nobel and the Peace Prize. We decided to teach our students about Alfred Nobel because every time we teach students about someone notable (MLK Jr., Malala, etc.), we love to tell students that they won something, such as the Nobel Peace Prize. However, we never teach kids what those prizes actually mean!

Briefly, Alfred Nobel did create the Nobel Prizes, but he also invented dynamite. That information might seem random, but many people believe that dynamite—and the great many casualties it caused—was actually one of the reasons why he invented the prizes. As the story goes, Alfred and his brother were working in a lab one day when an explosion killed his brother. The newspapers caught wind of this story and ran it, but they got their information wrong. They printed a scathing article that ridiculed Alfred Nobel for being the "merchant of death" and said that *he* had died by explosion! Alfred Nobel read this and was devastated. He could see what the world would say about him after his death, and was not happy about it. While it's never been proven, it's been heavily speculated that he did not want that to be his legacy, so he divided his fortune into what would eventually become the Nobel Prizes.

We found this information absolutely fascinating. After we taught our students about him, you can believe that for the rest of the year whenever we read a book that mentioned someone winning the Nobel Prize, we had kindergarten students exclaim, "Hey, that's that guy you taught us about who wanted to say sorry for hurting people and he made the prize!" This is what we mean when we say the more authentic, real, and global the content we give our students, the more connections happen. Our brains are hardwired to find connections. That's how we make sense of the world and learn.

At a planning meeting one day, LaNesha looked up an image of the Nobel Peace Prize, and began to study it. A coworker glanced over and said, "Oh! I have a little trophy you can have if you are teaching about this award." The next day, she came to the classroom with a three-inch-tall trophy, placed it on LaNesha's desk, and walked out. Within seconds, students were swarming the tiny trophy.

"What is that?" one student said, intensely eyeing the trophy.

"How do we win it? Who are you giving it to?" said another student.

This was obviously something they were really into, so LaNesha started to lean in. "What do you guys think it is for?" They began to speculate. Then she asked them why they wanted it so badly. See where we're headed? Sociology. What is it about trophies and medals that makes people want them so badly?

"Why do you all want this?"

"Because we want to win!"

"What if you won, but there was no trophy?"

"That would be okay, I guess . . . but we want the trophy."

"But why?"

"Well, because when we look at it, it will remind us that we won something and we will feel proud!"

Now we were getting somewhere. "Ohhh, okay. So, feeling proud of yourself makes you feel good. And this award would be a way to remind yourself to feel good. But where do people keep their awards?"

"My uncle loves to bowl and he has a cabinet full of trophies behind a glass wall! We are not allowed to touch it or we get in BIG trouble!"

"Why do you think he doesn't want anyone to touch it?"

"Well, because if we touched it, we could break it or lose it, and then he wouldn't be able to look at it and feel proud of himself anymore."

Bam. That was it. People love to have awards to feel proud of themselves. People also like to keep their awards in special places so that they are able to remember how they felt. A STEM project was born. A project that would have an authentic, global connection. A meaningful project that would allow us, the educators, to stand back and watch without feeling like the class was only having fun without any learning going on.

The kids were given the task of creating a structure that could hold an award or trophy. We grabbed the tape and the flexi straws. We printed

photographs of various ways that awards could be displayed, and we told the students to work in teams to engineer the perfect stand to hold the Nobel Peace Prize. We went through the engineering process just like a regular project, but there was so much more purpose and intentionality behind it than in the past. Not only was there an understanding of who Nobel was, but they also took care to design a stand that looked nice because they understood the sociology (and importance) behind displaying physical awards. Cracking this code opened the door for everything else when it came to STEM.

History and STEM

Later that month, we learned about the Roman god Janus because it is said that he is where the name January comes from. Janus, the god of passages, is a two-headed mythological being with one head that looks to the past and one that looks to the future. We discussed this history, and through a series of conversations, we of course arrived at the globe. We talked about where all of this originated, and we ended up looking up photographs of Rome. We eventually saw pictures of the Roman Colosseum, and that's when the questions began to roll in:

"What is that building?"

"Why is it broken down?"

"Why are there so many windows?"

"Who went there? What did they do there?"

"Why did they have to have so many seats?"

They wanted answers! On and on it went until we were bullied (in the best way) into researching facts about the Colosseum in our free time. As we looked at the pictures, we became really intrigued with the structure. Structure! There it was: potential for a STEM challenge!

We printed lots of pictures of the Colosseum and posted them in the block area. When the students came in the next day, we told them that their challenge was to work as a team to create a Colosseum that could hold the most seats. They were so excited to take this on because they understood what this place was used for. They worked together to create tiered seating. One group ran out of arch-shaped blocks and got upset. Then one of them asked if they could go next door and ask the other kindergarten class to borrow their arched blocks! They were so engaged. This STEM challenge was fun and powerful for them as they had the background knowledge to truly engage with the content.

Examples like these are hidden everywhere, just beneath the surface. We simply have to think a little differently about the content we are working with.

Hidden Figures and STEM

When we study scientists, it's really easy to connect it to a STEM project! After we saw the movie *Hidden Figures*, we also read books, watched videos, and studied the brilliant women featured in the motion picture.

Too many times, the "M" in STEM typically gets ignored, so we decided to focus on Katherine Johnson, one of the human computers who worked for NASA. She was able to execute extremely complex equations with stellar accuracy. We read a book that said that when she was a little girl, she would count everything, all the time. We thought that a counting challenge would be fun! We created cards with lots of stars on them, and passed them out to groups.

The challenge was to tell exactly how many stars were on the cards. This proved more challenging than it might sound. In groups, the students had to count the tiny stars printed all over four cards, which required strategy, precision, and accuracy. While we were working, we asked students why we were doing this project. Most of them replied with something like, "Because Katherine was a good counter, so we are trying to be good counters too!" That's what we were after. That's solid gold, right there.

Another scientist, Mary Jackson, was known for her work with wind tunnels. She tested models with wind blasts up to twice the speed of sound! Her work was instrumental in predicting how spaceships would hold up in extreme conditions. After learning about her life and legacy, we thought her work was an obvious choice to turn into a STEM experiment. Students worked in groups to create spaceships using toilet paper rolls, aluminum foil, construction paper, and glue. Then they were then given a specific amount of tape to use to secure their rockets. From there, the rockets were tested at various wind speeds (with a blow dryer!). The scientific process ensued.

Culture and STEM

We learned about the first person of color to integrate the NBA, Wataru Misaka, and what that meant for him as a Nisei (second-generation Japanese American) during the time just after Pearl Harbor. We looked up early pictures of the NBA and talked about what it might have felt like to be the first and only Japanese player in the league.

Naturally, the topic of basketball came up quite a bit. "He must have been really good at basketball because he played in the NBA!" one student shared. That opened up a conversation about how one becomes skilled at something. We talked about practicing and truly understanding what you are trying to achieve, then we watched videos of basketball players shooting baskets from different parts of the court. As we were watching, we started paying attention to the ball going into the net. We had an idea: what if we could pull in the famous catapult experiment to launch basketballs to specific spots on a court?

Almost on the spot as the video was playing, we began to draw students' attention to the arcs that the ball made as it flew into the net. We noted how some of the paths were high and some were lower. The students didn't realize it, but they were being set up for their STEM challenge! The students learned some vocabulary terms, and we experimented with strategies for achieving the perfect arc to get a ball to land on the right spot on the backboard. We even used the slow-motion feature on a cell phone to record the launches! While students watched the playback, they used some old transparency paper to trace the paths of the balls' arcs. Then, they labeled them with an H for high or an L for low.

While we can't expect kindergarteners to have mastered physics, we can make them familiar with a concept that might appear later on in their education. As we completed this STEM challenge, we were able to step back, and think, "Yes. Now we're launching things with purpose."

We didn't worry that we'd have to cringe if an adult came into the room to ask the students what they were doing, as they'd say, "Launching stuff!" We actually hoped someone would come and visit so the students could explain that we'd learned about a man that was a fantastic basketball player and that you have to consider the angles you use to get the ball in the basket. They were using teamwork, collaboration, and innovation, but those components of learning were seamlessly connected to the content that they were learning about through social studies. Now when we study any cultural figure, we are always thinking about scientific connections that can be turned into STEM lessons.

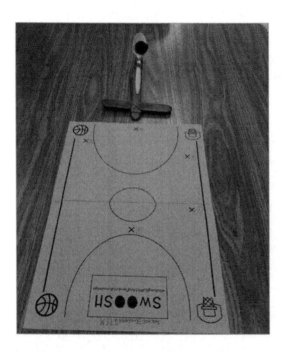

Gingerbread and STEM

Remember those Not Your Average Units we walked through before? Here's another snapshot of how we took a theme—gingerbread—and made it global through STEM. We were looking for something to go beyond the gingerbread science that we always see: gingerbread cookies dissolving in water. Typically, teachers read beloved gingerbread literature, where the fate of the poor gingerbread man lies with the fox crossing a river. This is where the gingerbread-dissolving-in-water experiment stems from. That's fun, but we knew that if we dug a little deeper, there was something else that could be done. We discovered that there is an actual residential architecture style called gingerbread. This style originated in Haiti, and it is gorgeous. That is interesting enough in itself, but as we researched these homes, we read that after the catastrophic earthquake hit Haiti in 2010, these gingerbread homes were some of the only structures that remained standing!

This definitely piqued our interest. We looked up the architects who designed the buildings and learned all about Léon Mathon, Joseph-Eugène Maximilien, and Georges Baussan—three men who were largely responsible for these homes. This was such a fun opportunity to celebrate Haiti and talk about what great engineers those men must have been to create buildings that were so sturdy. Never knowing what might light a spark in our students, we decided to attempt to be as great as those Haitian architects and build a structure that could withstand a simulated earthquake.

Teams of students worked together to build toothpick-and-marshmallow towers that would be inserted into trays of Jell-O (thank you, parent volunteers!). The goal was for the towers to remain standing for thirty seconds. A STEM challenge with a focus like that can translate into children caring about problems that happen in the world—like earthquakes—and immediately springing into action to solve them.

Look around. What's happening in the world that you can connect to your unit? For instance, consider how long Puerto Rico was without electricity after Hurricane Maria. What if we approached our electricity unit through this lens? How engaged would students be if they realized what it would be like to live months and months with absolutely no power? Would they lean in a little closer to try and see what the "big deal" is about electricity? Maybe this could plant seeds in some students who might grow up to create new ways of ensuring that power is not so easily lost.

We also love a good volcano science experiment. What about when we saw people quite literally fleeing for their lives during the eruption of Kilauea in 2018? A unit on volcanoes could be powerful if we intentionally began it with an element of humanity in our STEM projects.

UNPACK

Instead of teaching a math or science lesson that your students won't ever need or use, add meaningful elements of the real world to your STEM challenges.

IMPACT

Students will learn how math, engineering, and science connect to the ways we actually live, giving a human context to technology.

CHAPTER SEVEN

GLOBAL PERSPECTIVE THROUGH BOOKS

Raise your hand if you don't have time for social studies and you tell yourself you'll just squeeze it into your reading block here and there when you remember to. This used to be us as well! We began to select picture books that would lend themselves to social studies connections in order to squeeze more socials studies content into our days.

When we first started teaching, social studies was the black sheep of the school-subject family. Reading, writing, and math were the family favorites, and that's all we were told to focus on—with a little science sprinkled in if we had time. No one else we worked with, veteran or rookie, taught social studies. It just didn't seem important to anyone. Even administrators didn't seem to care what was happening in the world of social studies as long as reading, writing, and math were being taught well.

With the exception of a holiday here and there, social studies was largely ignored in our first few years in the classroom. We were laser focused on becoming the best reading teachers we could be. Every now and then we felt a little guilty for ignoring social studies and not

showing science the love it deserved, but we convinced ourselves that if we could teach our students how to read, they could learn about history on their own time or focus on it in the upper grades, where it seemed more important.

We wish now we had combatted this very wrong way of thinking by asking ourselves, "What foundation are we giving these kids to set them up for success in those upper grades?" We know that a strong foundation is key in any subject area, whether that's reading, math, or writing. We make sure to equip our students with the skills they need before sending them on to the next grade level in other areas. Why should social studies be an exception?

Our students deserve to be exposed to a variety of social studies topics and discussions well before they make it to middle school or high school. What if we told you that instead of putting it on the back burner, putting the responsibility on a teacher somewhere down the academic road, or squeezing it into reading once in a blue moon, you can purposefully integrate social studies into your reading block in a meaningful way daily?

Remember back in Chapter 2 when we told you that your students need windows and mirrors in their literature? In the article, "Mirrors, Windows, and Sliding Glass Doors," Dr. Rudine Sims Bishop teaches us that children from dominant social groups have always found their mirrors in books but have suffered from the lack of availability of books about others. They need these books as windows into reality, not just imaginary worlds. They need books that will help them understand the multicultural nature of the world they live in and their places as members of just one group as well as their connections to all other humans.

In this country, where racism is still one of the major unresolved social problems, books may be one of the few places where children who are socially isolated and insulated from the larger world can meet people unlike themselves. If they see only reflections of themselves, they will grow up with an exaggerated sense of their own importance and value in the world—a dangerous ethnocentrism.

A big Common Core reading shift that completely changed the game for us was the component that explains the importance of helping our students build their knowledge through the use of nonfiction texts. The Common Core State Standards Initiative website describes three shifts that teachers have been asked to make. The third, "building knowledge through content-rich nonfiction," states that

> Students must be immersed in information about the world around them if they are to develop the strong general knowledge and vocabulary they need to become successful readers and be prepared for college, career, and life. Informational texts play an important part in building students' content knowledge. Further, it is vital for students to have extensive opportunities to build knowledge through texts so they can learn independently.
>
> In K–5, fulfilling the standards requires a fifty-fifty balance between informational and literary reading. Informational reading includes content-rich nonfiction in history/social studies, sciences, technical studies, and the arts. The K–5 standards strongly recommend that texts—both within and across grades—be selected to support students in systematically developing knowledge about the world.[1]

For most of our entire teaching careers, building background knowledge has always been emphasized, but we'd never seen it implemented in a way that made sense. Luckily, in the middle of both of our school years, our administrations asked us to focus on building background knowledge for our kids. When we were chatting one evening, we realized that we could help each other roll out this new shift in a way that felt right for us and would also help our students make connections and acquire new knowledge that they could apply to the real world. It

---

1 Common Core State Standards Initiative, "Key Shifts in English Language Arts," accessed August 30, 2020, www.corestandards.org/other-resources/key-shifts-in-english-language-arts/.

would also be knowledge that would help them understand the complex fictional texts we were reading. For example, if we were going to read the book *The Boy Who Harnessed the Wind*, then we would need to ensure that students had some schema around windmills and how they work as well as the setting of the story: Malawi, Africa. These concepts are paramount in understanding what a windmill would mean for this community. Without a basic understanding of such concepts, the students might lag in their comprehension of the story.

First things first: instead of looking at the standards and picking a book that would just hit one or two focus standards for the week, we began looking for complex, rich texts that we could really dive into and guide our students through. We began to choose texts that were one to two grade levels higher than our students' current grade level. The reasoning behind this was that we did not want them to be able to read the book or hear the story and completely comprehend all of its elements from day one.

We wanted to make sure that they were acquiring new vocabulary words, picking up on themes and character motivations, learning and applying background knowledge to make sense of problems and events in the stories, and also being exposed to different perspectives that they would benefit from in their everyday lives. We began to look for books and started to compile a list of titles. While getting these titles together, we paid close attention to the books' settings and the characters' cultural backgrounds to ensure that the reading lessons could also be strong social studies lessons.

Finding a nonfiction text that supports your fictional story is key. This is also a great way to keep the balance between fiction and nonfiction in the classroom. It helps students see the importance of informational texts and how we can use them to pull out real information about the world. It also helps them see how to apply information to make sense of the events that occur in fiction stories.

We kept pushing ourselves to make sure we were offering our students different perspectives through picture books—in the *primary* grades. These conversations do not have to wait until students enter the intermediate grades!

We want to share the format we follow for building these reading lessons and encourage you to give our format a try for a week with your students. It might feel like a lot, but it's worth it. It starts before the lesson:

1. Choose a book that is one to two levels above your students' grade. It should be a picture book that they could not read and comprehend on their own. Try to choose a title that highlights a new culture, a different part of the world, an unknown tradition or holiday, or diverse characters that you can call attention to.

2. Pull a few vocabulary words from the text that are vital for your kids to be familiar with before they hear the story. Think of an engaging way (like pictures or motions to attach to the words) to get students to remember the words' meanings.

3. Think about the background knowledge your students will need to fairly and equitably access the text. It may be one topic; it may be more. This background knowledge may come in the form of a nonfiction text, a video, or a discussion. Even a YouTube video can help students with their background knowledge.

4. Think about the best chart to co-create *with* your students to capture their thinking. You might use a KWL chart, a flow map, a Venn diagram, or a bubble map. It is important that you do not create the chart on your own and show it to your students later. When you do that, it is just a poster, not an anchor chart. We tell students that these charts help capture and support their thinking across the week.

5. Create a focus for each day of reading the text, and cover all of the standards by the end of the week. If you pick a complex text, one book will hit most, if not all, standards.

6. Create a culminating task for students to complete by the end of the week. It should be something that shows their understanding of the text. It could be a debate, presentation, quiz, project, or the like. Try to switch it up as much as possible so students can show their understanding in a variety of ways.

Here's an example from one of our lessons: we chose the book *The Empty Pot* by Demi. This is a book for second graders, so it was above our kindergarteners' grade level. Set in China, this delightful story is about an emperor looking for a successor. He tells all the children in his kingdom to plant the seeds that he has given to them, then he tells them to "bring them their best" in one year's time. When the year passes, the children all return with gigantic plants to present to the emperor. Only one child, Ping, brings an empty pot. He tried everything he could to get the plant to grow, but nothing worked. But what the children don't know is that the emperor had actually cooked the seeds! They were unable to sprout. In the end, Ping is awarded the kingdom because he had integrity when the rest of the children chose to engage in manipulation to produce a plant.

Whew! There were many themes that needed to be unpacked in this text. We intentionally pulled out the vocabulary words *emperor*, *ashamed*, and *tended*. These are words that didn't have many context clues and were also important for our students to know in order for the events occurring in the story to make sense.

We taught these words to the kids on day one of the lesson, a day before we started reading the book. They were also reviewed in a different way each day to make sure the definitions weren't forgotten. Arguably the most important practice that we find absolutely necessary is to take time to build background knowledge. We read the book on our own and decided that the question we wanted our students to be able to answer by the end of it all was "Why is it important to have integrity?" We knew that before reading the text they needed to know and be able to understand three things:

1. What is integrity?

2. How do seeds grow and what might stop them from growing?

3. What is an emperor and why would anyone in China want to be one?

We typically spend one day building background knowledge. That isn't a hard-and-fast rule. Sometimes, you have to follow the needs of the text. This was necessary when we read *The Empty Pot*. We spent three days before we opened the book learning about those topics to build background. We covered one topic per day because it was critical to students' comprehension. Imagine the lost comprehension if our students didn't know that seeds won't grow if they are cooked. Similarly, if we hadn't taken the time to dig into the concept of an emperor, then students may not have realized exactly how high the stakes were. If they couldn't properly identify what it means to have integrity, it may have been difficult to understand why Ping had an empty pot.

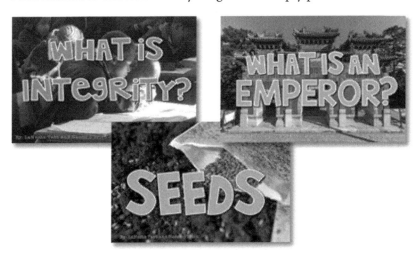

We read about these topics and created charts to capture students' thinking after engaging in discussions. We were at the map, of course. We also posted the anchor charts from our discussions in the room each day to make sure students would be able to refer back to them when it came time for us to read the text and use the knowledge to aid in the full comprehension of the story. It seems crazy, but all of this seriously was worked on before we opened the text. By this time, the students were dying to know what the story was about and ready to use their knowledge of emperors, integrity, and seeds. They'd already begun throwing the word *integrity* around with each other as if it had been a part of their vocabularies since birth.

"You took my pencil? You have no integrity."

"I saw you running in the hallway when you thought no one was watching. You need some integrity."

"I found this dollar that isn't mine, so I'm giving it to the teacher because I have integrity."

We hope you see the importance of building background knowledge. It's just as critical as reading and comprehending the text. It's needed *for* comprehending the text. It is important to build this foundation if we expect all students to be able to access the text. And it's a meaningful way to include social studies. Did you catch how we did that? We explored China and learned about emperors and how they ruled China for two thousand years. That's geography, history, and sociology right there! We also learned that emperors were extremely rich, which reminded the students about Mansa Musa (whom we had learned about during social studies earlier that year). That started a mini-debate about who was richer. They also wanted to know, of course, where China was in comparison to us and Mali, where Mansa Musa was from. This stuff gets their attention and stays with them in a way we've never seen before.

It was also a time to clear up a misconception in our classroom that one of our classmates was from China just because he was Asian. He was actually from Vietnam. We hopped back to the map and found Vietnam. We discussed how all Asian countries are not the same and that they have their own languages, people, customs, and ways of doing things. You may be thinking that these lessons are all over the place and this sounds like one too many interruptions. They aren't too many. And they are the *best* kinds of interruptions. They are interruptions from students eager to learn more about the world around them.

During the story, capture students' thinking and questions. Encourage them to take notes or draw pictures to remember key details (we like to use dry-erase boards). Ask preplanned reading questions that assess student comprehension but also infuse elements of social studies into the mix. Use the Common Core Standards as a guide. Break them apart into chunks that make sense, and have a new focus each day for understanding the text. Allow turn and talks and authentic discussion of the book to occur. Monitor and address any confusion or misconceptions. Encourage students to use co-created charts and their story notes to answer questions. Keep your culminating task in mind and monitor how student skills are progressing. Reflect on the lesson and adjust the following lesson as needed to guide students.

Here's an example from the lesson about *The Empty Pot*: We created a new anchor chart and map each day, including the background information, so that students could constantly refer back to them, which they definitely did. These charts should stay up all week long. The maps captured information about emperors, integrity, seeds, characters and settings, the sequence of the story, lessons learned, characters' feelings, and comparing and contrasting. Students also take notes (on dry-erase boards or in notebooks) through words, drawings, or symbols throughout the reading of the text to support later discussions.

We planned out and typed up our questions for each day, making sure to rely on the depth and complexity icons as a guide (more about those later). Each day, the questions were derived from one to two standards we wanted to focus on and build student mastery around. The questioning went from basic to more complex within a daily lesson as well as over the entire time spent on the book.

We remind students that the purpose of this discussion is to understand the text as much as possible and to see if we can pull any lessons from it to use in our real lives. Some of the questions (again, this is all preplanned) were intended to be answered on a dry-erase board, and some were planned turn and talks. It is the most amazing thing to hear students discussing texts independently. They would get up and refer to the anchor charts we'd created together earlier that week.

Students had the opportunity to share their answers aloud and defend their positions with evidence from the text. Other students always had the opportunity to agree or disagree and offer evidence of their own to support their thinking. So all of that sounds great—students are doing the majority of the thinking and heavy lifting and learning is happening!—but what are *you* doing? During this time, you are capturing thoughts and discussion gems on the anchor chart. You are popping into students' groups to add to their conversations, push their thinking, or get them started if they seem stuck or confused. Share answers or correct misconceptions for the good of the group. Make connections to social studies topics and pose questions for students to consider. As you visit groups, refer back to co-created anchor charts and student notes to encourage evidence-based answers.

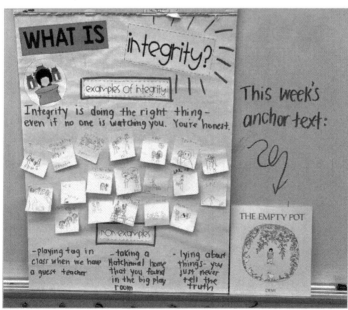

Depth and Complexity

Have you ever used the depth and complexity icons with your students? We mentioned earlier that these informed the questions we created for our students to answer. Once we introduced these icons to them, it changed the way we asked questions in our classrooms. These critical thinking tools were developed by Dr. Sandra Kaplan. When we plan a lesson, we use the icons to push ourselves to design more in-depth and complex questions to ask our students about a text or lesson.

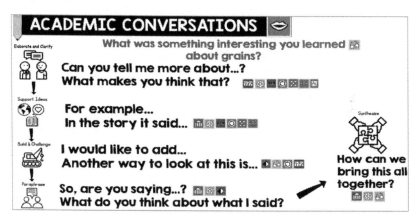

We also place the icon that the question is rooted in next to the question we're asking. The icon serves as a visual prompt to let the students know what type of thinking is being required of them. In order to

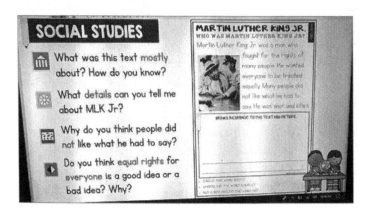

get to this level, we have to teach each icon first as well as the type of thinking it represents.

There are eleven icons in all. We definitely use some way more than others, but they always serve as great visual reminders to help students understand our content at a deeper level. The icons include:

- Language of the discipline
- Unanswered questions
- Rules
- Patterns
- Details
- Big ideas
- Ethics
- Trends
- Multiple perspectives
- Across disciplines
- Change over time

We also intentionally seek to offer students a different perspective in our lessons through the characters and settings of the books that we choose. We've seen many teachers use the same books—"classics" or otherwise—year after year. These books typically only showcase white characters or animals.

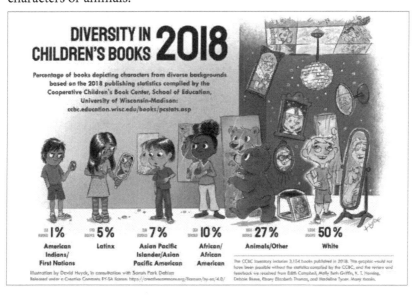

From what we have seen, it seems that only very rarely are students exposed to different cultures, races, and ethnicities in books. Books that do that, if introduced to students at all during the school year, are sometimes relegated to certain times of the year to fit into a holiday or celebration of some sort—never simply to be enjoyed as literature. It can be hard for some people to branch out and change up what they've done every year of their teaching careers, but it's so worth it for our students to have their perspectives widened and to learn more about other corners of our culturally diverse world. We can use reading with social studies to do just that.

Put It All Together Now

After your class has taken the time to build all of the amazing background knowledge, review the vocabulary words, have daily discussions, and create anchor charts, your students will be able to show what they know. Our absolute favorite way to do this is through a friendly class debate.

Keep in mind the story of *The Empty Pot*: The old Chinese emperor was looking for someone to take his place after he passed on. He gave all of the children in the land flower seeds and told them to come back in a year and show him their best. The main character, a boy named Ping, tries all year to get his seed to produce something, anything, but it just won't grow. Remember? Good.

On a Friday morning, in a neutral tone, we made this statement to our first graders: it was okay for the children in the story to cheat and switch their seeds because they really wanted to be the next emperor. This is where background knowledge about emperors came in handy. The students realized how amazing it would be to become an emperor and understood why Ping was stressing out. A year passes and all the children go back to see the emperor. Everyone has an amazing flower to show the emperor, except for poor Ping. Ping is all embarrassed and even begins crying, but then the author, Demi, hits us with a plot twist: the emperor had cooked all of the seeds before handing them out!

This is where our background knowledge about seeds came in handy. We knew that seeds that have been exposed to extreme heat or cold would not grow. Then how did all of the other kids have these beautiful flowers to show off? The emperor had actually tricked everyone to see who had integrity.

In that moment, all of our students realized they had just seen an example of integrity, even though the word isn't mentioned anywhere in the book. What's really funny is that earlier in our reading, when Ping's plant wasn't growing, a few of the students suggested that he get a flower from the store and pretend that he grew it! Ha—no integrity at all!

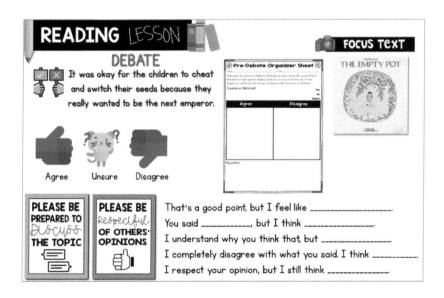

So, back to the debate. We asked our kids to agree or disagree that it was okay for the children to cheat and switch their seeds because they really wanted to be the next emperor. We also gave our students the option to be unsure. We gave them debate-planning sheets, and they made their choices. They jotted down reasons to support their stance as well as brainstormed what their classmates might come up with to support an opposing stance. Students got up to check out our co-created anchor charts, then headed back to their seats to add information we'd discussed and built over the course of the week. We discussed the rules of debating and set four in place:

1. Be prepared to discuss the topic.
2. Be respectful of others' opinions.
3. Listen and make eye contact with your peers (if you can).
4. Rephrase the last statement that was made before talking.

We also gave them some sentence stems to work with:

- That's a good point, but I feel like _____.
- You said _____, but I think _____.
- I understand why you think that, but _____.
- I completely disagree with what you said. I think _____.
- I respect your opinion, but I still think _____.

After the students finished filling out their debate sheets, they spread out into three groups: the group that agreed with the statement, the unsure group, and the group that disagreed. We sat out of the way. We made the statement out loud, and almost all of our students shot their hands into the air, waving their debate sheets wildly. We wish we could capture the energy and enthusiasm of the students in the room with words. You just had to be there.

Sure, we could have created an assessment that asked: Who was the main character? What was the setting? What was the problem and what was the solution? How did Ping feel in the middle of the story? Why? But we assessed all of that and then some during our debate. If our students didn't know the characters in the story, it would come up during the debate. We didn't need to ask about the problem or the solution, because our students were here debating about it.

> "Well, of course the other kids cheated! Do you know how important it is to be an emperor in China?"

"But we all know cooked seeds can't grow. It didn't matter what the kids did. That's not fair for the emperor to do!"

"I still disagree that they should have cheated. You have to have INTEGRITY! That's why Ping won and the emperor chose him."

"Well, I think the emperor didn't have integrity because he kind of lied to the kids. Why would the emperor of China do that?!"

Students used example after example from the text to make points and counterpoints. They used the vocabulary words too. They walked over to our anchor charts to point out what it meant to have integrity and argued that cheating is wrong no matter what. Some argued that cheating was okay if the price was right; after all, emperors are extremely rich! Students switched sides as evidence swayed them to change their minds. The unsure kids suddenly became sure, while a few others suddenly became unsure as evidence was placed in front of them to grapple with. One of the students brought up a great point: "Wait a minute. Did all of those kids' parents know they cheated? Did they help them cheat? My mom would never help me cheat! Can grown-ups cheat?"

We were able to use this to connect our students to a real-life event that was happening in the country. Felicity Huffman, Lori Loughlin (a.k.a. Aunt Becky from *Full House*), and others had been in the news around this time because of the college-admissions scandal in which thirty-three parents were accused of cheating the system to get their kids accepted. We discussed this, and wouldn't you know, the word *integrity* (or lack thereof) was thrown around some more.

The principal, the dean of instruction, and a reading coach stopped by to listen in on the debate. They couldn't believe that these first graders were debating in this manner using text-based evidence to support their thinking. A student's grandmother stopped Naomi in the hall later that week to report that her grandson could not stop talking about this debate and wanted her to read the book so he could debate with her at home! This was our second debate of the year, and we had more to come. They got better with each one. Can you picture yourself doing this in your classroom? We hope you can. We KNOW you can.

UNPACK

Strategically use reading lessons to incorporate social studies and widen your students' perspectives about the world every day. Be intentional about the books you choose. Choose books like they matter—because they do.

IMPACT

Students will not only gain new context for these books but also learn new vocabulary and other skills, such as problem solving and debating.

CHAPTER EIGHT

FINAL THOUGHTS, TIPS, AND STRATEGIES

W e'd like to leave you with this final chapter as a trouble-shooting guide of sorts. We often hear from educators who tell us that they are motivated and excited but also SCARED. We get it. Let's process.

No, We Don't "Sneak" Critical Lessons In

"Your lessons are great, but how do you teach them without the parents finding out?" This question, and many similar ones, are asked from time to time. They come from well-meaning teachers who are inspired to impart social studies to their students but aren't sure how their students' parents and guardians or school administrators will feel about the content they are teaching. They want to know how we "sneak" in the critical lessons that they agree all students would benefit from.

We want to let you in our secret. The best way that we have figured out **how to** address keeping our lessons a secret is that we don't! We

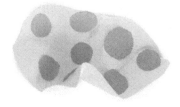

don't shut the doors, raise our right hands, and swear our students to secrecy. In fact, it's quite the opposite. We are very up-front and honest about what we will be diving into each school year. We both send home our own letters to parents to let them know that we will be diving into cultures—our own, as well as those of people from around the globe.

For social studies, including lessons about racial and social justice, we send home monthly newsletters detailing what we'll be learning about and encouraging our students' parents and guardians to continue the conversation at home. We tell them that there are issues impacting people around the world that our students will grow up to be a part of and that we will be analyzing those issues and brainstorming ways to solve them. Students need to know about the world so that they can become better citizens of it. It sounds cliché, but they literally are our future leaders.

We let parents and guardians know that their students will be engaging in lessons and discussions about history, sociology, economics, geography, and civics. It's exciting to share all of the amazing topics we will be covering over the course of the year. We want our parents and guardians to know what their kids are up to. Not only that, we are sure to make our administrators aware of our content. Teachers are able to handle just about anything with the support of their administrators. If your administration team is aware and supports you, it will remove a whole layer of anxiety! We are both fortunate to not have had too much pushback, and to have had supportive administrators. Through our blog and social media, we have heard from other educators who are not as fortunate. What we suggest is to be open and honest. Communicate with your parents and administrators about the shifts you'd like to make and see what everyone is comfortable with. You may not be able to achieve huge changes overnight, but Rome wasn't built in a day.

What if you think your administration wouldn't support these shifts? Use wisdom. If you teach in a community that has not engaged in this type of work, have a plan. Schedule meetings with your administration and explain the intent and importance of the work. You might bring a sample text or an article for people to peruse. Talk through a sample lesson or conversation prompt. Be prepared to remind them that your goal is not to teach students *what* to think but rather to teach students *how* to think. We aren't in the business of "changing minds" or "indoctrination." We are in the business of giving students opportunities to grapple with big ideas, consider multiple perspectives, and engage in civil discourse. They will need that to make decisions for our future.

What Are Your State's Standards?

The National Council for the Social Studies reminds us that social studies is intended to promote civic competence. Unfortunately for K–5 teachers, the Common Core State Standards don't have any clear social studies standards mapped out. They are said to be embedded in the K–5 reading standards. Most states have a version of social studies standards, but we know teachers who have said that their schools have never even looked at them! This leaves it up to teachers—who usually have little to no extra time to plan in-depth lessons—to squeeze social studies into reading and just hope for the best.

Find out if your state has standards, and start planning meaningful lessons. Check out the standards for older grades and see what you can scale back to use to meet your grade-level needs. If you find that the standards are proving to be problematic (i.e., "celebrating" Columbus vs. learning about actual historical events), guess what? That's great! *Teach it.* Teach whatever the standard is—and then flip it! Find the missing perspectives that can be taught alongside the topic. You might teach the typical Columbus narrative and then balance it with a study on Indigenous Peoples' Day. Tell the students why the controversy exists. Ask them to share their opinions on it. Maybe you are teaching an older grade and you are tasked with covering a topic like the California Gold Rush and it is feeling extremely traditional. Again, you might teach the traditional approach but then ask your students where the missing narratives are and send them out to reclaim them! Presidents' Day? Constitution Day? Great! Teach them. Then, discuss the other stakeholders who were involved in the building of this country. Ask students why they think such narratives were left out of history lessons in the past. Ask them who benefits from the narrative presented and who might have something different to say about it.

Collect questions that can give students a wider understanding of an event and the people involved. Those questions might sound like:

- What year(s) are we learning about? What else was happening in the world at this time that might have affected these events?
- Where did this event happen? Who else lived in surrounding areas? What did those people contribute?
- Do I see myself represented in this event? If I were alive then, what would I have been doing?
- What were people who do not look like me doing?

Those questions can send students into a whole new world of interesting facts that will begin to make that traditional history more relatable, equitable, and accurate. This doesn't have to be an overwhelming task. Even if you focused on one question and did a quick whole-group inquiry over a few days, you have now illustrated to your students that history is not, and has never been, one-sided. You never know—your students' thirst for uncovering facts from history could grow into future professions as researchers or historians. Keep in mind that it is challenging to switch up our habits of teaching a single narrative because it requires some unlearning on our parts. We are often learning right alongside the students—but that's why it's so invigorating! That type of energy is infectious. It trickles down to students when they are engaged in real, authentic learning.

So, while we wish the standards were better, they are great for some much-needed unlearning. Remain standards-based. Use them, but rethink the learning. Reroute the teaching.

Help! I Only Teach a Concentrated Subject Area

Maybe you're reading this wishing you could fit social studies into your subject area, but you're wondering how because you teach music, physical education, technology, or math exclusively. While we haven't had experience teaching only one subject area, we have had to challenge ourselves to bring social studies into other subject areas like science, math, and reading. If you're teaching a math lesson about counting, perhaps you could tie another culture into your lesson. Add some social studies flair to it! Consider the history of the math concept, or maybe approach the sociological aspect of how that concept affects the way people live today.

What if instead of your typical counting lesson, you took the time to teach your kids how to pronounce the numbers in a different language? Bonus points if it's the home language of a student in class and they get to teach their peers. You can show your students math strategies from a different country or even the different characters or math tools people from other countries use with their students. We are always looking for opportunities to widen students' views of the world. And who knows, you and your students might discover that the strategies that work in a different country are actually more helpful than the strategies provided by your own curriculum. Remember: different people do different things in different ways, and that's okay. If we want to make a social studies connection in a subject outside of social studies, sometimes we will set a timer for two minutes. Then, we'll read a short paragraph or show a photograph about the topic. We'll think aloud. We'll pose a question. We try to always have things like this in our back pockets for those little empty times in the day that can be filled with something interesting.

We've seen our students learn how to play football in physical education classes. The coach broke down the lessons over the course of a week, teaching the rules and how to pass, kick, and catch. The students finally ended the week by playing a game of football. If these students didn't learn football at school, there's a good chance they would have the opportunity to be exposed to it at recess with friends, at an after-school club, or on Sundays at home with their families. What if instead of football, basketball, and old-school dodgeball, students were taught bossaball from Spain, caber toss from Scotland, Muay Thai from Thailand, or gostra from Malta? Yes, you might teach a concentrated area, but remember this: if you teach humans, you teach social studies.

Present Facts

An important component in any lesson is the information being presented. It is vital that the information put in front of students to discuss or debate is 100 percent factual. Our opinions should never be taught as fact. If we are charged with teaching our students history, sociology, economics, and so on, we must stick to what is true. We strive to make certain that all of the information we put in front of our students to take in and analyze is the truth. In order to accomplish this, we do a lot of research.

You might think, "But doesn't that take a lot of time?" It does. But the alternative is to continue the cycle of biased or flat-out incorrect lessons—and we can't do that. If we, as educators, don't begin to turn the tides, who will? How long are we supposed to wait? How many classes must we graduate? Will we have to wait until the textbook companies get on board and release accurate and comprehensive historical accounts? What if that never happens? At some point we have to admit that it's on us to do what we can. If your math textbook incorrectly stated that you should teach students that $1 + 1 = 5$, would you teach that? Or would you correct it? None of us will be perfect and get it all right. Of course not! But the very nature of our profession is to impart knowledge. Knowledge knows no textbook limits. Knowledge is not shackled to a single narrative that must be maintained. Knowledge is boundless.

So, yes. We have to double-check and triple-check our sources to make sure we are giving our students accurate accounts and telling real stories about the past. We want to tell our students stories that aren't always told. We don't want to simply regurgitate the same old social studies lessons that we grew up with. We'll remind you again: When we present facts, we are not teaching students what to think. We are teaching students how to think. We offer a chance for students to gain critical thinking skills, engage in civil discourse, and find ever-important perspective. Perspective is the breeding ground for empathy.

Remain Unbiased

When the time comes to present your lessons to your students, they will have questions. Your students may also want to know your thoughts about a topic or which side you'd choose in a debate. For the sake of the learning environment, and in an effort to allow your students to truly process the information presented to them themselves, it's important to remain unbiased.

As the presenter of the information as well as the facilitator of classroom discussions, you have to be an objective party. As much as possible, we have to keep our feelings and personal beliefs out of our social studies lessons. This includes facial expressions! Let students come to their own conclusions after you've presented them with enough facts. When students question you, you can always turn the question over to another student in class or let them know you need more information before you form an opinion on the matter at hand. Our favorite phrase during debates with kids is, "Hmm, I'm not sure. What do you think?"

Invite Them In

Don't teach lessons you're ashamed of. The lessons you put together should be well researched, well thought out, and something you know is helping your students develop their discourse about what truly matters.

We personally loved inviting our teaching coaches and vice principals into our lessons to help facilitate discussion among our students. Giving students information about the world is not something we should have to sneak in. For us, these lessons are as vital as teaching our students how to read and solve equations.

We once had a kindergarten student whose grandparent reached out to the school and asked for their grandchild to not participate in any more of our social studies lessons. The reason for this was because she didn't like that her granddaughter was learning about Ruby Bridges and the conversations, feelings, and questions that came with learning about segregation. We responded the same way we would have if a parent didn't want their child to receive phonics lessons or learn how to add. All of our lessons are valuable and necessary to be successful in the real world, and we want all of our students to be present for each and every one. We believe in this work that we set out to do.

We requested a meeting with the grandparent, and the next day, we were able to talk face to face and reach a point where this grandparent felt comfortable moving forward with her granddaughter in the classroom. The issue was more about how uncomfortable she felt continuing the conversations at home than it was about the lesson per se. When the meeting was finished, this grandparent agreed that these lessons were critical for her grandchild to be a part of and that accurate history was more important than feel-good history. We also let her know we could chat more at any time and that she was always welcome to sit in on a lesson to see how we hold discussions in class.

She was very reassured by that conversation, saw the benefits of the lessons, and wanted her grandchild to continue participating in our social studies discussions and activities. She was even thrilled to know Naomi would be her grandchild's first grade teacher because she looped up with her students the following year. It was an opportunity to have a meaningful conversation with a guardian and advocate for a student's right to learn accurate history.

We understand that this approach might be difficult. Like we mentioned earlier, you may have to take smaller steps. You know your administrators, parents, and community best. You may have success by compiling a few lessons and letting your administrators know what you'd like to present, how you will present it, and what you hope your students will gain from it. Also—we cannot stress this enough—front-loading will save you from so much. If you know the topic will be a little controversial, make administration and parents aware *before* you teach it. Invite them to preview the text ahead of time. Send samples from books or lessons home if you can. Invite questions and curiosity.

LaNesha

I typically lay a groundwork for this at our back-to-school night, showing slides of work and topics covered in the past. My room is covered in beautifully diverse picture books that night. I want the books to send a message: we will do our best to explore the world this year. None of my lessons come out of left field. A parent might have a problem with something you think is perfectly fine, so build relationships with families in order to facilitate dialogue.

I can recall getting a message from a teacher that had read a book in class that was about the World Trade Center attacks of September 11. The teacher was devastated when a parent called her furious for teaching students about September 11. While we can all have our own thoughts and opinions about that parent's response, what remains true is that if the parent had been made aware that the topic would be discussed *ahead of time*, the entire situation might have gone more smoothly. Also, if a parent truly has that much of a problem (even after talking to you), then alternatives can be discussed with you and the family.

Your Students Aren't Too Young for These Topics

We hear this a lot: "I'm too scared to cover Martin Luther King Jr. because he was, you know . . . shot! I don't want my students to be sad." But why? It is sad. Whenever we hear this, we remember a quote from a man named Lawrence Tan, who said, "If children are old enough to experience injustice, then they are old enough to learn about it." These very sobering words wipe out any excuse for feeling like children are unable to process information or hold conversations.

Studies have demonstrated that children, even from even infancy, are able to understand concepts of race and even discriminate based on them. Data about preschool expulsions shows that nonwhite children are expelled at a much higher rate than their white counterparts. In LaNesha's family, in the year 2020, she had to console a nephew who came home saying that he wished he were "peach with spikey hair" so that he could play with a group of boys that told him he was "too dark" to play with them. In other words, young children can and do experience injustice. We all learn about injustice at a young age. Naomi recalls her first-grade niece being told she couldn't play with a few girls at recess because she didn't have "yellow hair and blue eyes" like them. This was in 2019. Whether or not students have the vocabulary to describe what they are experiencing or behavior they are engaging in, it's still happening. Why wouldn't we want to educate them about these important topics?

You know your students best. If we go back to the Dr. King example, just think that your students, or people they know, have more than likely had family members who have passed away. They may have heard about death on the news. You don't have to give every gory detail to let students know that someone lost their life. We certainly don't.

So hopefully by now you are excited to get into your classroom and start making some changes. But where do you start? What lessons are most important for you to dive into? Which traditional lessons can you tweak or get rid of completely? We've put together some ideas to help you get started.

Planning Out Your Days, Weeks, and Months

We think we can all agree—and hopefully we've convinced you with our stories—that meaningful and engaging social studies lessons for primary students are vital in helping to develop a foundation for good citizenship. Our learners don't stay little very long, and we are charged with the very important job of presenting lessons that will help them make informed decisions and live in a world that is culturally diverse.

For many years, we were under the impression that we did not have time in our schedules to devote to teaching social studies every day. In reality there was time; we just didn't want to give it up to devote to teaching social studies. Do you think it's important enough to make time for?

Naomi's lessons were thirty minutes a day. Sometimes longer when the class was in the middle of a heated debate or on a virtual trip on the other side of the world. Then they'd all rush down to the lunchroom and apologize for being tardy, still discussing the culture that they learned about in that day's sociology lesson. LaNesha had to employ the "get in where you fit in" strategy with her lessons. This meant instead of playing a YouTube story while packing up for the day, maybe she shared a book or an event. Then, the next morning, when the students came in, one of their options for their morning activities related to that social studies topic. Social studies lived in her community-circle time. It looked like a book, video, or conversation prompt with a directive for students to turn and talk with their neighbors about it. Since we weren't going for mastery or grades in social studies (because we didn't have to at that time), it was all about exposure. Other teachers do have carved-out time in their schedules and do have to report grades—so the ability to do more is built in. Do what you can. Something is better than nothing.

Now, we are going to preach to the (newly social-studies-obsessed) choir that we hope you are ready to join after reading this book—so it might sound a little hopelessly optimistic. We're still gonna say it. Yes, we found ways to integrate social studies into reading, writing, math, and science when we could, but we believe that time solely focused on social studies is different. The subject deserves its own time. It has a different feel when it isn't being merely integrated but given space to be its own thing. It also sends the message to kids that this work is important. We understand that this is not the reality for many educators—but we still want it to be!

So maybe you have to start small and designate one day a week to an impactful social studies lesson. Our guess is that you'll soon discover this one day is simply not enough—for you or your kids. Add in more days as you begin to see just how much you and your students need these lessons and as you get more efficient at planning them! Get out a calendar and plan out what you and your students want to cover and how many days each lesson might last. If a month is too much, focus on just a week. Think about the books you may need from the library, the videos you can show on the internet (if you have access), and the questions you can pose to get your students critically thinking about the world. Let's make it happen. Let's make *something* happen. We promise, the only regret you'll have is not starting this work sooner.

Now you're probably wondering about the time you'll need to plan these lessons. We know how precious a teacher's time is. It is sacred! When we were building this work, we were both full-time teachers with young children. Leisure time was not plentiful. Teaming up together to split the work helped us a ton. We did have to spend a collective one to two hours a week outside of our school day researching and creating ebooks, slideshows, experiences, and response sheets for our students. But the great thing is that once you have your first template or week planned, it's easy to plug in other topics you want to teach. If you have a team, maybe you could all work together to divide and conquer. If you don't have time to put together a short slide show of information you want to present, see if an already published book meets your needs. Search YouTube for a helpful video. You don't have to create a cute worksheet for students to show their thinking. You can simply get notebooks for everyone and have students write their responses about the new information they've learned and then share with their peers. You can pose a question on the board to get a debate going. It doesn't have to be perfect!

Just think to yourself: What could I be teaching daily to develop good citizens? Active citizens? Global citizens? Only integrating social studies is not enough. Would you only teach social studies and tell yourself that students don't need reading instruction because you read during social studies time? In this same regard, we must move away from thinking that we can truly give social studies the respect it deserves when it is confined to a reading passage a few times a month. We do recognize that a lot of this is due to a broken educational system. Certain subjects are given preference because they are scored on a test. *We get it.* We are just attempting to do what we can to make change on a level that we have access to.

The impact of primary teachers not teaching social studies (or teaching it poorly) is too significant to ignore. The impact of teaching it effectively and honestly is extremely powerful. It should be explored to the fullest with even the youngest of learners. A craft is cute, but is that what we want our social studies lessons to be reduced to?

And so, fellow educators, we ask you to do something that we do at the beginning of every school year: Reflect on lessons that you've taught in the past or will teach in the future. Unpack what your impact will be. What kind of students could we send out into the world if we decided to teach global lessons in kindergarten—and the first grade teacher got on board too? What if the second and third grade teachers joined in, and so on? What kind of thinkers and problem solvers would we have a hand in producing? Can you imagine it? At the end of your time with your students on their journey in K–12, will they be one step closer to becoming informed citizens, able to function in a culturally diverse society, with critical thinking skills and an in-depth knowledge about the world around them? We hope the answer is yes.

UNPACK

Consider why, when, and how you're going to start this work. Schedule the time for these lessons and be up-front about your purpose with parents and administrators.

IMPACT

You will inspire a generation of young minds to grow into engaged, informed citizens, able to contribute to a diverse global society in the future.

ACKNOWLEDGMENTS

Thank you to the amazing team of people that directly helped us every step of the way. We appreciate you more than words can say. Dave, Shelley, Sal, Marisol, and Tara, thank you for believing in us and working with us to put a book out into the world that we are in love with.

Naomi O'Brien

To my family, for cheering me on as I wrote this book. To the DBC, Inc. crew for making publishing my first book a dream come true. To my friends, who encourage me, pray for me, and believe in me. To my past students, who taught me so much and restored my faith in humanity on a daily basis. And to LaNesha Tabb, for bringing me on this incredible journey with you and being the best partner and friend a girl could ever ask for.

LaNesha Tabb

To my husband, David: You hold me together. Thank you for allowing me the space to walk in my purpose. Thank you for pushing me to be better. And thank you for being my very best friend.

To my children, Lillian and David Jr.: Thank you for letting Mommy take another call (AGAINNNN?) and have her laptop while we watch movies. I do this for you two.

To my dad, my mom, and Leah + Alex: Thank you for helping to mold me into the person that I am. I could not be doing what I get to do without your prayers and your support. Dad, thank you for being a teacher and an author first—I follow in your footsteps.

To my friends and colleagues: Thank you for rocking with me. I am so blessed to be able to do life with you all. Thanks for supporting and believing in me. Thank you to the Get Your Teach On team: you helped me find my voice and gave me a platform to share my work. Special thanks to the table of brainstorming ladies who helped us with the title of this book—especially our friend Abby.

To the DBC team: Thank you for your excitement and guidance on this project. Thank you for helping us tell our story. Thank you for hearing us.

To Naomi: Thanks for saying yes.

ABOUT THE AUTHORS

| Naomi O'Brien |

Naomi O'Brien has been working with kids and teaching students since 2002. She has been a licensed elementary school educator since 2010. Along the way, she's acquired an ESOL endorsement, a Gifted and Talented endorsement, and an Early Childhood Education endorsement. She loves being a teacher, she loves learning, and she loves helping students fall in love with learning. In the schools she has worked in, she is known for creativity, being tech-savvy, and incredible classroom management. Naomi prides herself on the way she builds relationships with kids and their parents/guardians, being culturally responsive, having high expectations for all students in an equitable way, and always being a learner. She doesn't ever teach the same thing the exact same way two years in a row because she always strives to improve her practice. She is a racial-justice advocate in and out of the classroom, and she believes informed students have the ability to change the world.

LaNesha Tabb

LaNesha Tabb is an apron-donning primary educator from Indianapolis, Indiana. She has served the past fourteen years in kindergarten through the third grade. She holds a bachelor's degree from Anderson University in Anderson, Indiana, and is a two-time Teacher of the Year awardee (2012 and 2019). LaNesha holds leadership roles at the district and school level as a lead learner for new initiatives. LaNesha is the content creator behind Education with an Apron, where she creates fresh and innovative teaching resources. When LaNesha is not in the classroom teaching kindergarten, she can be found speaking at education conferences all over the United States, sharing teaching strategies and ideas on her social media channels, and serving as a wife to David and mom to her two young children, Lillian and David Jr. LaNesha wholeheartedly believes that little children can do BIG things, have BIG thoughts, and carry out BIG conversations.

SPEAKING

Naomi O'Brien

Besides working directly with K-2 students, Naomi O'Brien educates teachers and parents about the importance of racial justice at home and in the classroom.

Popular Speaking Topics:

- Building a Culturally Responsive School
- Addressing Racism in the Classroom
- Centering Diversity and Inclusion with Picture Books
- The Importance of Social Studies in Primary Grades
- Navigating Critical Conversations with Kids

Naomi O'Brien can be found on social media at @ReadLikeaRockStar. There she shares resources and invites others to learn alongside her to become anti-racist educators and people.

LaNesha Tabb

LaNesha Tabb is a full-time kindergarten teacher, but when she's not in the classroom, you can find her delivering keynote addresses and presenting workshops for school districts and various conferences all over the United States and Canada. LaNesha's current classroom experience allows her to provide an authentic and impassioned voice to the topics that she is called to speak to. Because of her years of teaching and creating resources, LaNesha can share a powerful message to primary teachers everywhere: little kids can do big things!

Popular Speaking Topics:

- Make Social Studies Important Again
- Culture in the Classroom
- Reimagine Reading: Infusing Diverse Literature across Multiple Subjects
- All Children Can Write
- Thematic Units Like Never Before
- Social Studies and STEM
- Self-Care for Educators: What Happens after the Bubble Bath?

LaNesha Tabb can be contacted for engagements on her website, LaNeshaTabb.com, and she can be found on social media at @apron_education.

MORE FROM
DAVE BURGESS Consulting, Inc.

Since 2012, DBCI has been publishing books that inspire and equip educators to be their best. For more information on our titles or to purchase bulk orders for your school, district, or book study, visit DaveBurgessconsulting.com/DBCIbooks.

Like a PIRATE™ Series
Teach Like a PIRATE by Dave Burgess
eXPlore Like a Pirate by Michael Matera
Learn Like a Pirate by Paul Solarz
Play Like a Pirate by Quinn Rollins
Run Like a Pirate by Adam Welcome
Tech Like a PIRATE by Matt Miller

Lead *Like a PIRATE*™ Series
Lead Like a PIRATE by Shelley Burgess and Beth Houf
Balance Like a Pirate by Jessica Cabeen, Jessica Johnson, and Sarah Johnson
Lead beyond Your Title by Nili Bartley
Lead with Appreciation by Amber Teamann and Melinda Miller
Lead with Culture by Jay Billy
Lead with Instructional Rounds by Vicki Wilson
Lead with Literacy by Mandy Ellis

Leadership & School Culture
Culturize by Jimmy Casas
Escaping the School Leader's Dunk Tank by Rebecca Coda and Rick Jetter

Fight Song by Kim Bearden

From Teacher to Leader by Starr Sackstein

If the Dance Floor Is Empty, Change the Song by Joe Clark

The Innovator's Mindset by George Couros

It's OK to Say "They" by Christy Whittlesey

Kids Deserve It! by Todd Nesloney and Adam Welcome

Let Them Speak by Rebecca Coda and Rick Jetter

The Limitless School by Abe Hege and Adam Dovico

Live Your Excellence by Jimmy Casas

Next-Level Teaching by Jonathan Alsheimer

The Pepper Effect by Sean Gaillard

The Principled Principal by Jeffrey Zoul and Anthony McConnell

Relentless by Hamish Brewer

The Secret Solution by Todd Whitaker, Sam Miller, and
   Ryan Donlan

Start. Right. Now. by Todd Whitaker, Jeffrey Zoul, and
   Jimmy Casas

Stop. Right. Now. by Jimmy Casas and Jeffrey Zoul

Teachers Deserve It by Rae Hughart and Adam Welcome

Teach Your Class Off by CJ Reynolds

They Call Me "Mr. De" by Frank DeAngelis

Thrive through the Five by Jill M. Siler

Unmapped Potential by Julie Hasson and Missy Lennard

When Kids Lead by Todd Nesloney and Adam Dovico

Word Shift by Joy Kirr

Your School Rocks by Ryan McLane and Eric Lowe

Technology & Tools

50 Things You Can Do with Google Classroom by Alice Keeler and
   Libbi Miller

50 Things to Go Further with Google Classroom by Alice Keeler
   and Libbi Miller

140 Twitter Tips for Educators by Brad Currie, Billy Krakower, and
   Scott Rocco

Block Breaker by Brian Aspinall

Code Breaker by Brian Aspinall

Control Alt Achieve by Eric Curts

Google Apps for Littles by Christine Pinto and Alice Keeler

Master the Media by Julie Smith

Reality Bytes by Christine Lion-Bailey, Jesse Lubinsky, and Micah
  Shippee, PhD

Sail the 7 Cs with Microsoft Education by Becky Keene and
  Kathi Kersznowski

Shake Up Learning by Kasey Bell

Social LEADia by Jennifer Casa-Todd

Stepping Up to Google Classroom by Alice Keeler and
  Kimberly Mattina

Teaching Math with Google Apps by Alice Keeler and
  Diana Herrington

Teachingland by Amanda Fox and Mary Ellen Weeks

Teaching Methods & Materials

All 4s and 5s by Andrew Sharos

Boredom Busters by Katie Powell

The Classroom Chef by John Stevens and Matt Vaudrey

The Collaborative Classroom by Trevor Muir

Copyrighteous by Diana Gill

CREATE by Bethany J. Petty

Ditch That Homework by Matt Miller and Alice Keeler

Ditch That Textbook by Matt Miller

Don't Ditch That Tech by Matt Miller, Nate Ridgway, and
  Angelia Ridgway

EDrenaline Rush by John Meehan

Educated by Design by Michael Cohen, The Tech Rabbi

The EduProtocol Field Guide by Marlena Hebern and
  Jon Corippo

The EduProtocol Field Guide: Book 2 by Marlena Hebern and
  Jon Corippo

Instant Relevance by Denis Sheeran

LAUNCH by John Spencer and A.J. Juliani

Make Learning MAGICAL by Tisha Richmond

Pure Genius by Don Wettrick

The Revolution by Darren Ellwein and Derek McCoy

Shift This! by Joy Kirr

Skyrocket Your Teacher Coaching by Michael Cary Sonbert

Spark Learning by Ramsey Musallam

Sparks in the Dark by Travis Crowder and Todd Nesloney

Table Talk Math by John Stevens

The Wild Card by Hope and Wade King

The Writing on the Classroom Wall by Steve Wyborney

Inspiration, Professional Growth & Personal Development

Be REAL by Tara Martin

Be the One for Kids by Ryan Sheehy

The Coach ADVenture by Amy Illingworth

Creatively Productive by Lisa Johnson

Educational Eye Exam by Alicia Ray

The EduNinja Mindset by Jennifer Burdis

Empower Our Girls by Lynmara Colón and Adam Welcome

Finding Lifelines by Andrew Grieve and Andrew Sharos

The Four O'Clock Faculty by Rich Czyz

How Much Water Do We Have? by Pete and Kris Nunweiler

P Is for Pirate by Dave and Shelley Burgess

A Passion for Kindness by Tamara Letter

The Path to Serendipity by Allyson Apsey

Sanctuaries by Dan Tricarico

The SECRET SAUCE by Rich Czyz

Shattering the Perfect Teacher Myth by Aaron Hogan

Stories from Webb by Todd Nesloney

Talk to Me by Kim Bearden

Teach Better by Chad Ostrowski, Tiffany Ott, Rae Hughart, and Jeff Gargas

Teach Me, Teacher by Jacob Chastain

Teach, Play, Learn! by Adam Peterson

The Teachers of Oz by Herbie Raad and Nathan Lang-Raad

TeamMakers by Laura Robb and Evan Robb

Through the Lens of Serendipity by Allyson Apsey

The Zen Teacher by Dan Tricarico

Children's Books

Beyond Us by Aaron Polansky

Cannonball In by Tara Martin

Dolphins in Trees by Aaron Polansky

I Want to Be a Lot by Ashley Savage

The Princes of Serendip by Allyson Apsey

The Wild Card Kids by Hope and Wade King

Zom-Be a Design Thinker by Amanda Fox

33594463R00100